WNT AND β-CATENIN PATHWAY: FROM BASIC SCIENCE TO THERAPEUTIC APPLICATIONS

PROF (DR.) PHOOL CHANDRA

Made with ♥ on the Notion Press Platform
www.notionpress.com

Dedicated to My Beloved Mother and Father

Contents

Foreword

It is a great honor to pen the foreword for this exceptional book, "**Wnt/β-Catenin Pathway: From Basic Science to Therapeutic Applications**," authored by **Prof. (Dr.) Phool Chandra**. This scholarly work represents a significant contribution to the field of molecular biology and pharmacology, offering deep insights into one of the most critical signaling pathways that underpin both health and disease.

As Principal of Teerthanker Mahaveer College of Pharmacy at Teerthanker Mahaveer University, I have always been an advocate for advancing knowledge through rigorous research and scholarly discourse. This book exemplifies that commitment by bridging the gap between foundational scientific research and its therapeutic implications. The Wnt/β-Catenin pathway, as meticulously explored in this text, is a cornerstone of modern biology with far-reaching implications across various domains of medicine, including oncology, regenerative medicine, and metabolic disorders.

Prof. Chandra has done an outstanding job of distilling complex molecular mechanisms into a coherent and accessible narrative, making this book an invaluable resource for both seasoned researchers and students venturing into the field for the first time. The thorough exploration of the pathway's role in embryogenesis, tissue homeostasis, and disease pathology, coupled with discussions on the latest therapeutic strategies, positions this book as a critical reference for anyone involved in the study or treatment of diseases influenced by Wnt/β-Catenin signaling.

The forward-looking perspectives on personalized medicine, regenerative therapies, and the potential for novel drug development highlighted in this book are particularly timely. In an era where precision medicine is becoming the standard of care, understanding the intricacies of pathways like Wnt/β-Catenin is crucial for the development of targeted therapies that can revolutionize patient outcomes.

I congratulate Prof. (Dr.) Phool Chandra on this remarkable achievement. "Wnt/β-Catenin Pathway: From Basic Science to Therapeutic Applications" is poised to become an essential text in the field, guiding current and future research while providing a solid foundation for the development of innovative therapies.

Prof. (Dr.) Anurag Verma
Principal, Teerthanker Mahaveer College of Pharmacy
Teerthanker Mahaveer University
Moradabad, India

Preface

The Wnt/β-Catenin signaling pathway is a cornerstone of cell biology, playing critical roles in development, tissue homeostasis, and disease. Since its discovery, the pathway has garnered immense interest due to its intricate mechanisms and profound implications in both fundamental biology and clinical research. This book, *"Wnt/β-Catenin Pathway: From Basic Science to Therapeutic Applications,"* aims to provide a comprehensive exploration of the Wnt/β-Catenin signaling cascade, covering its historical context, molecular intricacies, and diverse roles in health and disease.

Historical Perspective

Understanding the Wnt/β-Catenin pathway requires an appreciation of its origins and evolution. The early discoveries that unveiled this pathway laid the foundation for subsequent research and therapeutic strategies. We trace the journey from the initial observations to the establishment of Wnt signaling as a central player in numerous biological processes.

Molecular Components and Mechanisms

This book delves into the detailed molecular components of the Wnt/β-Catenin pathway, including Wnt ligands, Frizzled receptors, β-Catenin, and the destruction complex. We provide an in-depth examination of both canonical and non-canonical signaling mechanisms and their regulatory aspects. By elucidating these molecular details, we aim to enhance understanding of how disruptions in these components can lead to disease.

Biological and Clinical Relevance

The role of Wnt/β-Catenin signaling in embryogenesis, tissue homeostasis, and regenerative medicine is explored in depth. From its pivotal role in stem cell maintenance and tissue renewal to its implications in cancer, metabolic disorders, and neurodegenerative diseases, this pathway is integral to a wide array of biological functions. Additionally, we highlight cutting-edge research on therapeutic strategies, including small molecules, biological therapeutics, and gene therapy.

Computational Modeling and Drug Discovery

Advancements in computational modeling have revolutionized our approach to studying complex signaling pathways. This book covers bioinformatics approaches, systems biology models, and predictive modeling techniques that aid in understanding the Wnt/β-Catenin pathway and facilitate drug discovery. These tools are essential for translating basic research into clinical applications and for developing targeted therapies.

Future Directions

As our understanding of the Wnt/β-Catenin pathway evolves, new questions and challenges arise. We explore emerging therapeutic strategies, unresolved questions, and the potential for personalized medicine. This book aims to provide insights into the future of Wnt signaling research and its impact on the field of medicine.

Acknowledgments

This book represents the collective effort of numerous researchers, clinicians, and academics who have contributed to the field of Wnt/β-Catenin signaling. We extend our gratitude to all the contributors who have provided their expertise and insights. Their dedication and passion for understanding this complex signaling pathway have been instrumental in shaping the content of this book.

Purpose and Audience

The primary goal of this book is to offer a comprehensive and accessible resource for researchers, clinicians, and students interested in Wnt/β-Catenin signaling. We aim to bridge the gap between basic science and clinical applications, providing a valuable reference for those engaged in research, drug development, and therapeutic interventions.

We hope that this book serves as a foundational resource for understanding the Wnt/β-Catenin pathway and inspires further exploration into its biological significance and therapeutic potential.

Author's Note

The complexity and breadth of the Wnt/β-Catenin signaling pathway necessitate a multidisciplinary approach to fully appreciate its impact. As we continue to unravel the intricacies of this pathway, we look forward to future advancements and discoveries that will further enhance our understanding and therapeutic capabilities.

Thank you for joining us on this journey through the Wnt/β-Catenin signaling pathway. We invite you to explore the chapters within and contribute to the ongoing dialogue in this exciting and rapidly evolving field.

Sincerely,

Prof (Dr.) Phool Chandra

Author, *"Wnt/β-Catenin Pathway: From Basic Science to Therapeutic Applications"*

Acknowledgements

I would like to express my deepest gratitude to the individuals whose support, guidance, and encouragement have been instrumental in the completion of this book.

First and foremost, I am profoundly grateful to the honorable **Shri Suresh Jain**, Chancellor, Teerthanker Mahaveer University, for his visionary leadership and unwavering commitment to fostering a vibrant academic environment. His dedication to excellence in education and research has been a source of inspiration throughout this journey.

I extend my heartfelt thanks to the honorable **Prof. V.K. Jain**, Vice-chancellor, Teerthanker Mahaveer University, whose continuous support and encouragement have been pivotal in driving forward the academic endeavors at our institution. His commitment to academic rigor and research innovation has provided a strong foundation for this work.

I am sincerely appreciative of **Dr. Aditya Sharma**, Registrar, Teerthanker Mahaveer University, for his efficient administration and unwavering support. His contributions have been invaluable in ensuring a conducive environment for academic and research activities.

I am also deeply indebted to **Prof. Manjula Jain**, Dean Academics, for her guidance and encouragement. Her leadership in academic affairs has played a crucial role in the development of this work, and her commitment to academic excellence continues to inspire.

My special thanks to **Prof. Anurag Verma**, Principal, Teerthanker Mahaveer College of Pharmacy, for his insightful suggestions and constant encouragement. His support has been instrumental in the successful completion of this book.

I would also like to acknowledge the valuable contributions of **Prof. Piyush Mittal**, Associate Dean (Research), whose expertise and dedication to research excellence have greatly influenced the quality and depth of this work.

Finally, I wish to express my deepest appreciation to **Prof. Neetu Sachan**, for her unwavering support, understanding, and encouragement. Her belief in my work and her patience during the long hours of research and writing have been invaluable.

To all of you, I express my deepest gratitude for your support, encouragement, and belief in this project. It is through your collective efforts and unwavering dedication to academic excellence that this book has come to fruition.

Prof. (Dr.) Phool Chandra

Section I: Foundations of Wnt/β-Catenin Signaling

Chapter 1: Historical Perspective of Wnt Signaling

The book begins with a historical overview of Wnt signaling, tracing its discovery and evolution. It highlights key research milestones that have shaped our understanding of this critical pathway.

Chapter 2: Molecular Components of the Wnt/β-Catenin Pathway

A detailed account of the core components of the Wnt/β-Catenin pathway, including Wnt ligands, Frizzled receptors, β-Catenin, the destruction complex, and TCF/LEF transcription factors. This chapter provides a thorough understanding of the molecular players involved in Wnt signaling.

Chapter 3: Mechanism of Wnt/β-Catenin Signal Transduction

Explores the canonical and non-canonical Wnt signaling pathways, detailing the mechanisms of β-Catenin regulation, pathway activation, and cellular responses.

CHAPTER ONE

Historical Perspective of Wnt Signaling

1.1 Discovery of the Wnt Pathway

The discovery of the Wnt signaling pathway is a fascinating journey that began in the early 1980s with studies in both cancer research and developmental biology. The name "Wnt" is derived from a combination of "Wg" (Wingless) and "int-1."

1.1.1 The Role of int-1 in Mouse Mammary Tumorigenesis

In 1982, Roel Nusse and Harold Varmus identified the gene *int-1* (integration 1) in mice while studying tumorigenesis. This gene was found to be activated by the integration of the mouse mammary tumor virus (MMTV) into the genome of host cells, leading to the development of mammary tumors. The *int-1* gene was later shown to be highly conserved across species, including humans, indicating its significant role in biology.

1.1.2 Discovery of the Wingless Gene in Drosophila

Around the same time, in the field of developmental biology, researchers were studying the *wingless* (Wg) gene in the fruit fly *Drosophila melanogaster*. This gene was essential for proper embryonic development, particularly in determining the segments of the developing fly. The *wingless* mutant flies had a characteristic loss of wings, hence the name.

1.1.3 Linking int-1 and Wingless

In 1987, it was discovered that *int-1* and *wingless* were homologous genes, meaning they shared a common evolutionary ancestor. This realization connected cancer research with developmental biology, leading to the coining of the term "Wnt" (a portmanteau of *Wg* and *int-1*), and marked the beginning of Wnt signaling as a significant field of study.

1.2 Evolutionary Significance of Wnt Signaling

Wnt signaling is an ancient and evolutionarily conserved pathway that plays a fundamental role in the biology of multicellular organisms.

1.2.1 Conservation Across Species

The Wnt signaling pathway is conserved from simple organisms like hydra and worms to more complex organisms such as humans. The pathway's core components, including Wnt ligands, Frizzled receptors, β-catenin, and TCF/LEF transcription factors, are found across a wide range of species, highlighting its evolutionary importance.

1.2.2 Role in Development and Evolution

The Wnt pathway is crucial for embryonic development in all animals. It regulates cell fate determination, patterning, and morphogenesis during the development of tissues and organs. The conservation of Wnt signaling components across species indicates that the pathway likely arose early in the evolution of multicellular organisms and has been maintained due to its essential role in developmental processes.

1.2.3 Evolution of Complexity

The complexity of the Wnt pathway has increased over time, with the expansion of Wnt gene families and the diversification of Wnt signaling mechanisms in more complex organisms. This has allowed the Wnt pathway to regulate a broader range of biological processes, contributing to the evolution of complex body plans and specialized tissues.

1.3 Overview of Wnt-Related Research Milestones

The study of the Wnt signaling pathway has been marked by several key discoveries and milestones that have advanced our understanding of its role in biology and disease.

1.3.1 1990s: Cloning of Wnt Genes and Pathway Elucidation

Throughout the 1990s, researchers cloned various Wnt genes from different species and began to unravel the components of the Wnt signaling pathway. Key discoveries included the identification of Frizzled receptors, Dishevelled proteins, and β-catenin as central players in the pathway.

The destruction complex, which controls β-catenin levels in the cell, was characterized during this period. This complex includes APC (adenomatous polyposis coli), Axin, GSK-3β (glycogen synthase kinase 3β), and CK1 (casein kinase 1). The understanding of how this complex regulates β-catenin stability and its subsequent role in gene transcription was a significant advancement.

1.3.2 2000s: Wnt Signaling and Disease

As the role of Wnt signaling in development became clearer, researchers began to focus on its implications in disease, particularly cancer. Mutations in Wnt pathway components, such as APC and β-catenin, were found to be drivers of cancer, especially in colorectal cancer. This period also saw the discovery of the pathway's involvement in other diseases, including osteoporosis, neurodegenerative diseases, and metabolic disorders. The link between Wnt signaling and stem cell biology was also established, with Wnt pathways being critical in maintaining the self-renewal and pluripotency of stem cells. This discovery has had significant implications for regenerative medicine.

1.3.3 2010s: Therapeutic Targeting of Wnt Pathway

The 2010s were marked by efforts to develop therapeutic strategies targeting the Wnt/β-catenin pathway. Researchers explored small molecule inhibitors, monoclonal antibodies, and other approaches to modulate the pathway in diseases such as cancer, fibrosis, and metabolic disorders. Advances in understanding the cross-talk between Wnt signaling and other pathways, as well as the identification of non-canonical Wnt signaling branches, further enriched the field.

1.3.4 Recent Advances

More recently, the development of advanced technologies like CRISPR-Cas9, high-throughput screening, and single-cell RNA sequencing has allowed researchers to study Wnt signaling with unprecedented precision. These tools have led to new insights into the pathway's role in cell differentiation, tissue regeneration, and its potential as a therapeutic target.

Conclusion

The historical development of Wnt signaling research reflects the pathway's pivotal role in both fundamental biology and clinical science. From its initial discovery through cancer studies and developmental biology to its current status as a key target in therapeutic development, the Wnt/β-catenin pathway continues to be a central focus of research with far-reaching implications for understanding health, disease, and evolution. This chapter sets the stage for a deeper exploration of the pathway's mechanisms, roles, and applications in subsequent chapters of the book.

CHAPTER TWO

Molecular Components of the Wnt/β-Catenin Pathway

The Wnt/β-Catenin signaling pathway is a highly regulated and complex cascade of molecular interactions. This chapter delves into the key molecular components that drive the pathway, explaining their roles and how they interact to control critical cellular processes.

2.1 Wnt Ligands

2.1.1 Structure and Classification

Wnt proteins are secreted glycoproteins that play a fundamental role in the Wnt signaling pathway. There are 19 different Wnt ligands in humans, all of which are characterized by their cysteine-rich structure, which is crucial for their stability and function. Wnt ligands are classified into canonical and non-canonical types based on their ability to activate the β-catenin-dependent (canonical) pathway or alternative signaling pathways.

2.1.2 Synthesis and Secretion

Wnt ligands are synthesized in the endoplasmic reticulum and undergo post-translational modifications, including palmitoylation, which is essential for their secretion and interaction with receptors. The enzyme Porcupine (PORCN) is critical in this modification process. Wnt proteins are then secreted from the cell via the action of the Wntless (WLS) protein, which ensures their transport to the cell surface for release into the extracellular environment.

2.1.3 Functions

Wnt ligands are key regulators of cell proliferation, differentiation, and migration during embryogenesis and adult tissue homeostasis. They also play a significant role in stem cell maintenance, tissue regeneration, and the immune response. Dysregulation of Wnt ligand production or secretion can lead to various pathologies, including cancer, fibrosis, and developmental disorders.

2.2 Frizzled Receptors and Co-Receptors (LRP5/6)

2.2.1 Frizzled Receptors

Frizzled (FZD) proteins are the primary receptors for Wnt ligands on the cell surface. There are ten different Frizzled receptors in humans, each containing a seven-transmembrane domain characteristic of G protein-coupled receptors

(GPCRs). The extracellular cysteine-rich domain (CRD) of Frizzled receptors is responsible for binding Wnt ligands, initiating the Wnt signaling cascade. Upon Wnt ligand binding, Frizzled receptors undergo conformational changes that facilitate the recruitment of Dishevelled (DVL) proteins, which are key intracellular mediators of Wnt signaling.

2.2.2 Co-Receptors LRP5/6

Low-density lipoprotein receptor-related proteins 5 and 6 (LRP5/6) are co-receptors that work in conjunction with Frizzled receptors to propagate the Wnt/β-catenin signal. LRP5/6 contains extracellular domains that interact with both Wnt ligands and Frizzled receptors, stabilizing the receptor-ligand complex and enhancing signal transduction. The cytoplasmic tail of LRP5/6 undergoes phosphorylation, creating docking sites for Axin, a component of the destruction complex. This process is crucial for inhibiting the destruction complex and stabilizing β-catenin.

2.2.3 Functions and Significance

The Frizzled-LRP5/6 receptor complex is central to the initiation of the canonical Wnt signaling pathway, leading to the activation of downstream targets that regulate cell fate decisions. Mutations or aberrant expression of Frizzled receptors or LRP5/6 can result in impaired Wnt signaling, contributing to diseases such as osteoporosis, cancer, and metabolic disorders.

2.3 β-Catenin and Its Role

2.3.1 Structure and Localization

β-Catenin is a multifunctional protein that plays a dual role in cell adhesion and gene transcription. It consists of an N-terminal domain, a central armadillo repeat domain, and a C-terminal domain. In the absence of Wnt signaling, β-catenin is primarily localized in the cytoplasm and is tightly regulated by a destruction complex that targets it for degradation.

2.3.2 Regulation by the Destruction Complex

When Wnt signaling is inactive, β-catenin is phosphorylated at specific serine and threonine residues by the destruction complex, leading to its ubiquitination and subsequent degradation by the proteasome. The destruction complex prevents the accumulation of β-catenin in the cytoplasm, thereby inhibiting its entry into the nucleus and preventing the activation of Wnt target genes.

2.3.3 Role in Gene Transcription

Upon Wnt pathway activation, the destruction complex is inhibited, allowing β-catenin to stabilize and accumulate in the cytoplasm. It then translocates to the nucleus, where it interacts with TCF/LEF transcription factors to initiate the transcription of Wnt target genes. These target genes are involved in various processes, including cell proliferation, differentiation, and survival. β-Catenin's role as a transcriptional co-activator is central to its function in Wnt signaling.

2.3.4 Implications in Disease

Abnormal stabilization of β-catenin, often due to mutations in APC or β-catenin itself, can lead to uncontrolled cell proliferation and tumorigenesis, as seen in colorectal cancer. β-Catenin also has roles beyond Wnt signaling, such as in cell-cell adhesion where it interacts with cadherins, contributing to tissue architecture and integrity.

2.4 Destruction Complex (APC, Axin, GSK-3β, CK1)

2.4.1 APC (Adenomatous Polyposis Coli)

APC is a tumor suppressor protein that is a core component of the destruction complex. It binds to β-catenin and Axin, facilitating the phosphorylation of β-catenin by GSK-3β and CK1. APC mutations are commonly associated with familial adenomatous polyposis (FAP) and sporadic colorectal cancers, leading to impaired degradation of β-catenin and constitutive Wnt signaling activation.

2.4.2 Axin

Axin serves as a scaffold protein in the destruction complex, bringing together APC, GSK-3β, CK1, and β-catenin to promote β-catenin phosphorylation and degradation. Axin is a rate-limiting component of the complex, and its availability tightly controls the activity of the destruction complex. Axin is also regulated by post-translational modifications, such as phosphorylation and ubiquitination.

2.4.3 GSK-3β (Glycogen Synthase Kinase 3β)

GSK-3β is a serine/threonine kinase that phosphorylates β-catenin at specific residues, marking it for ubiquitination and proteasomal degradation. GSK-3β also phosphorylates Axin and APC, modulating their interactions and the overall activity of the destruction complex.

2.4.4 CK1 (Casein Kinase 1)

CK1 is another kinase in the destruction complex that phosphorylates β-catenin at the N-terminal serine/threonine residues, priming it for subsequent phosphorylation by GSK-3β. CK1 also phosphorylates LRP5/6 in the context of Wnt signaling activation, contributing to the inhibition of the destruction complex.

2.4.5 Function of the Destruction Complex

The destruction complex plays a critical role in maintaining low levels of β-catenin in the absence of Wnt signaling, thus preventing the inappropriate activation of Wnt target genes. The regulation of the destruction complex is a crucial control point in Wnt signaling, with implications for both normal cellular functions and pathological conditions.

2.5 TCF/LEF Transcription Factors

2.5.1 Structure and Function

TCF (T-cell factor) and LEF (lymphoid enhancer-binding factor) are transcription factors that bind to β-catenin in the nucleus to regulate the expression of Wnt target genes. TCF/LEF proteins contain a high-mobility group (HMG) box that allows them to bind to specific DNA sequences in the promoters of target genes. They also possess β-catenin binding domains, enabling their interaction with β-catenin.

2.5.2 Role in Wnt Signaling

In the absence of Wnt signaling, TCF/LEF factors are bound by co-repressors such as Groucho/TLE, repressing Wnt target gene expression. Upon Wnt pathway activation, β-catenin displaces the co-repressors and converts TCF/LEF from transcriptional repressors to activators, leading to the transcription of genes involved in cell proliferation, differentiation, and survival.

2.5.3 Diversity of TCF/LEF Family

The TCF/LEF family consists of four members in humans: TCF1, LEF1, TCF3, and TCF4. Each member has distinct expression patterns and functions, contributing to the specificity and diversity of Wnt target gene regulation in different tissues and developmental stages.

2.5.4 Implications in Disease

Dysregulation of TCF/LEF activity, whether through mutations or aberrant β-catenin signaling, can contribute to the development of cancers and other diseases. For instance, TCF4 is frequently implicated in colorectal cancer. The interplay between TCF/LEF factors and other transcriptional regulators adds an additional layer of complexity to Wnt signaling, influencing the outcome of the pathway in different cellular contexts.

Conclusion

The molecular components of the Wnt/β-Catenin pathway form a tightly regulated network that controls a wide range of cellular processes. Each component, from the Wnt ligands to the TCF/LEF transcription factors, plays a crucial role in ensuring the proper transmission of signals that dictate cell fate decisions. Understanding these components and their interactions provides critical insights into how the pathway functions in both normal physiology and disease states, setting the foundation for therapeutic interventions targeting Wnt signaling.

CHAPTER THREE

Mechanism of Wnt/β-Catenin Signal Transduction

This chapter explores the detailed mechanisms of Wnt/β-Catenin signal transduction, focusing on the canonical Wnt signaling pathway, its non-canonical counterparts, and the regulation of β-catenin stability and activity.

3.1 Canonical Wnt Signaling Pathway

The canonical Wnt signaling pathway, also known as the Wnt/β-catenin pathway, is the most well-characterized and studied branch of Wnt signaling. It plays a crucial role in regulating gene expression and controlling various cellular processes, including development, proliferation, and differentiation.

3.1.1 Initiation of Signaling

The canonical Wnt signaling pathway is initiated when a Wnt ligand binds to a Frizzled receptor and its co-receptor, LRP5/6, on the cell surface. This interaction is highly specific, with different Wnt ligands binding to distinct combinations of Frizzled and LRP5/6 receptors, thus providing a level of pathway specificity.

3.1.2 Formation of the Signalosome

Upon Wnt ligand binding, the cytoplasmic tail of LRP5/6 undergoes phosphorylation by kinases such as CK1 and GSK-3β. This phosphorylation event creates docking sites for the scaffold protein Axin, leading to the formation of a multi-protein complex known as the signalosome. The recruitment of Axin to the plasma membrane results in the disassembly of the β-catenin destruction complex (which includes APC, Axin, GSK-3β, and CK1), thus preventing β-catenin from being phosphorylated and targeted for degradation.

3.1.3 Stabilization and Accumulation of β-Catenin

With the destruction complex inhibited, β-catenin is no longer phosphorylated and marked for ubiquitination. As a result, β-catenin accumulates in the cytoplasm and eventually translocates into the nucleus.

3.1.4 Nuclear Translocation and Gene Activation

Once in the nucleus, β-catenin interacts with TCF/LEF transcription factors, displacing co-repressors such as Groucho/TLE and converting TCF/LEF into transcriptional activators. This leads to the activation of Wnt target genes involved in a variety of biological processes, such as cell cycle regulation, stem cell maintenance, and differentiation. Key target genes include *c-Myc*, *Cyclin D1*, *Axin2*, and *MMP7*.

3.1.5 Role in Development and Disease

The canonical Wnt signaling pathway is essential for embryonic development, tissue homeostasis, and regeneration. However, dysregulation of this pathway, particularly through mutations in components like APC, β-catenin, or Axin, is associated with several diseases, including cancer (notably colorectal cancer), bone density disorders, and fibrosis.

3.2 Non-Canonical Wnt Signaling Pathways

In addition to the canonical Wnt/β-catenin pathway, Wnt ligands can activate non-canonical pathways that do not involve β-catenin. These pathways regulate processes such as cell movement, polarity, and calcium homeostasis and are particularly important in development and tissue morphogenesis.

3.2.1 Wnt/Planar Cell Polarity (PCP) Pathway

The PCP pathway regulates the orientation and arrangement of cells within a tissue plane, crucial for processes like convergent extension during embryonic development. Upon Wnt ligand binding, Frizzled receptors activate the Dishevelled (DVL) protein, which in turn activates downstream effectors such as Rho GTPases (RhoA, Rac1) and the kinase JNK (c-Jun N-terminal kinase). This signaling cascade leads to cytoskeletal rearrangements that drive changes in cell shape and polarity, influencing the directional movement and alignment of cells.

3.2.2 Wnt/Ca^{2+} Pathway

The Wnt/Ca^{2+} pathway modulates intracellular calcium levels, which act as a secondary messenger in various cellular processes, including gene expression, cell adhesion, and motility. Activation of this pathway typically involves Wnt ligands binding to Frizzled receptors and G-protein-coupled receptors, leading to the release of calcium from intracellular stores. Calcium signaling then activates various calcium-sensitive proteins such as PKC (protein kinase C), CaMKII (calcium/calmodulin-dependent protein kinase II), and calcineurin, which mediate downstream effects.

3.2.3 Wnt/ROR2 Pathway

This non-canonical pathway involves the receptor ROR2 (receptor tyrosine kinase-like orphan receptor 2) and is associated with the regulation of cell movement and morphogenesis. ROR2 can interact with both canonical and non-canonical Wnt ligands, influencing cytoskeletal dynamics and cell migration. The pathway is implicated in developmental processes and diseases such as skeletal disorders and cancer.

3.2.4 Functions and Significance

Non-canonical Wnt signaling pathways are essential for the fine-tuning of cellular behavior during development and tissue repair. They often work in conjunction with canonical signaling, providing additional layers of regulation. Dysregulation of non-canonical Wnt pathways is linked to a variety of disorders, including congenital malformations, neurodegenerative diseases, and cancer metastasis.

3.3 Regulation of β-Catenin Stability and Activity

The regulation of β-catenin is central to the control of the Wnt/β-catenin pathway, as its levels and activity determine the transcriptional output of Wnt signaling. This regulation is achieved through a complex interplay of phosphorylation, ubiquitination, and proteasomal degradation.

3.3.1 Destruction Complex and β-Catenin Degradation

In the absence of Wnt signaling, β-catenin is kept at low levels in the cytoplasm through continuous degradation by the destruction complex. The destruction complex, comprising APC, Axin, GSK-3β, and CK1, phosphorylates β-catenin at serine and threonine residues near its N-terminus. Phosphorylated β-catenin is then recognized by the E3 ubiquitin ligase β-TrCP, which ubiquitinates β-catenin, marking it for proteasomal degradation.

3.3.2 Wnt-Dependent Inhibition of β-Catenin Degradation

When Wnt signaling is activated, the destruction complex is inhibited through the phosphorylation of LRP5/6 and the recruitment of Axin to the plasma membrane, away from the cytoplasmic complex. This inhibition prevents β-catenin phosphorylation, allowing it to escape degradation, accumulate in the cytoplasm, and eventually enter the nucleus to activate target gene transcription.

3.3.3 Nuclear Regulation and Transcriptional Activity

β-Catenin's role is not limited to its stabilization in the cytoplasm; its transcriptional activity is also tightly regulated within the nucleus. β-Catenin interacts with TCF/LEF transcription factors to drive the expression of Wnt target genes. However, this activity is modulated by co-factors and co-repressors that can either enhance or suppress transcriptional output depending on the cellular context. Post-translational modifications, such as acetylation and phosphorylation, can also influence β-catenin's interaction with nuclear partners, thereby regulating its transcriptional activity.

3.3.4 Feedback Mechanisms

The Wnt/β-catenin pathway is subject to multiple feedback loops that ensure precise control of β-catenin levels and activity. For example, *Axin2*, a key component of the destruction complex, is a direct target of β-catenin/TCF-mediated transcription. The induction of *Axin2* creates a negative feedback loop that limits Wnt signaling intensity. Other negative regulators, such as DKK (Dickkopf) proteins and sFRPs (secreted Frizzled-related proteins), act extracellularly to inhibit Wnt signaling by blocking Wnt ligand-receptor interactions.

3.3.5 Implications for Disease

The regulation of β-catenin is crucial for maintaining cellular homeostasis. Dysregulation, often due to mutations in components of the destruction complex or β-catenin itself, can lead to constitutive Wnt signaling and contribute to the development of cancers, particularly those with hyperactive β-catenin, like colorectal cancer. Therapeutic strategies targeting β-catenin stability and activity are being explored as potential treatments for Wnt-related diseases, including inhibitors of the β-catenin/TCF interaction and modulators of the destruction complex.

Conclusion

The Wnt/β-catenin signaling pathway is a complex and tightly regulated system that plays a critical role in cell fate determination, tissue homeostasis, and disease. Understanding the mechanisms of signal transduction, including the canonical and non-canonical pathways and the regulation of β-catenin, is essential for deciphering the broad impact of Wnt signaling in both normal physiology and pathological conditions. This chapter provides a comprehensive overview of these mechanisms, laying the groundwork for subsequent discussions on the pathway's implications in health and disease.

Part II: Biological Roles and Clinical Implications

Chapter 4: Role of Wnt/β-Catenin in Embryogenesis

Discusses the critical functions of Wnt/β-Catenin signaling in embryonic development, including axis formation, organogenesis, and cell fate determination.

Chapter 5: Wnt Signaling in Tissue Homeostasis

Examines the role of Wnt/β-Catenin signaling in maintaining stem cell populations, tissue renewal, and its specific functions in the gastrointestinal tract, skin, and hair follicles.

Chapter 6: Wnt/β-Catenin and Cancer

Analyzes the dysregulation of Wnt/β-Catenin signaling in cancer, covering mechanisms of pathway aberration, associated cancers, and potential therapeutic strategies.

Chapter 7: Wnt/β-Catenin in Metabolic Disorders

Investigates the connection between Wnt signaling and metabolic disorders such as obesity and diabetes, including its role in adipogenesis and lipid metabolism.

Chapter 8: Wnt/β-Catenin in Neurodegenerative Diseases

Details the involvement of Wnt/β-Catenin signaling in neuronal development and maintenance, and its implications in neurodegenerative diseases like Alzheimer's and Parkinson's.

Chapter 9: Wnt/β-Catenin and Bone Health

Explores the role of Wnt/β-Catenin signaling in bone formation, remodeling, and its implications in bone diseases such as osteoporosis.

CHAPTER FOUR

Role of Wnt/β-Catenin in Embryogenesis

Wnt/β-Catenin signaling plays a pivotal role in embryogenesis, governing critical processes such as axis formation, organogenesis, tissue patterning, and cell fate determination. This chapter provides an in-depth exploration of how the Wnt/β-Catenin pathway contributes to these essential developmental events.

4.1 Axis Formation

Axis formation is one of the earliest and most fundamental events in embryogenesis, establishing the basic body plan of the developing organism. The Wnt/β-Catenin signaling pathway is crucial in defining the anterior-posterior axis, as well as influencing the dorsal-ventral and left-right axes.

4.1.1 Anterior-Posterior Axis Formation

The anterior-posterior axis is established early in development and is heavily influenced by gradients of signaling molecules, including Wnt proteins. In many species, such as Xenopus (frogs) and zebrafish, Wnt/β-Catenin signaling is activated in the posterior region of the embryo. This gradient is essential for posteriorizing signals that establish the head-tail axis. Wnt signaling promotes the expression of posterior markers such as *Hox* genes, which are crucial for segmental identity along the body axis.

4.1.2 Dorsal-Ventral Axis Formation

The Wnt/β-Catenin pathway is also involved in dorsal-ventral axis specification. In vertebrates, Wnt signaling is typically higher on the dorsal side, contributing to the formation of dorsal structures, such as the neural tube and somites. This dorsally restricted activity of Wnt signaling is often regulated by inhibitors like DKK1 and Noggin, which are expressed on the ventral side, ensuring proper axis formation.

4.1.3 Left-Right Axis Formation

Wnt/β-Catenin signaling also plays a role in the establishment of the left-right axis, although this role is less direct compared to the other axes. The pathway interacts with other signaling cascades, such as Nodal signaling, to establish left-right asymmetry, which is crucial for the proper positioning of internal organs.

4.1.4 Role in Evolution

The role of Wnt signaling in axis formation is highly conserved across species, indicating its fundamental importance in embryonic development. Studies in various model organisms, including Drosophila, zebrafish, and mice, have highlighted the evolutionary conservation of this pathway in defining body axes.

4.2 Organogenesis and Tissue Patterning

The process of organogenesis, where organs and tissues are formed and patterned, is tightly regulated by Wnt/β-Catenin signaling. This pathway coordinates the spatial and temporal development of tissues, ensuring that cells differentiate into appropriate cell types and that organs are correctly positioned and formed.

4.2.1 Neural Development

Wnt/β-Catenin signaling is critical for the formation and patterning of the central nervous system (CNS). During neural development, Wnt signaling regulates the proliferation of neural progenitor cells, their differentiation into neurons, and the patterning of the neural tube. In the developing brain, Wnt signaling controls the formation of distinct brain regions, such as the forebrain, midbrain, and hindbrain, by regulating the expression of region-specific genes.

4.2.2 Limb Development

Limb development is another key process influenced by Wnt/β-Catenin signaling. Wnt signaling regulates the outgrowth and patterning of limbs by controlling the expression of key developmental genes like *Shh* (Sonic hedgehog) and *Bmp* (Bone morphogenetic protein). The pathway also coordinates the formation of the apical ectodermal ridge (AER) and the zone of polarizing activity (ZPA), two critical signaling centers that direct limb development.

4.2.3 Heart Development

The Wnt/β-Catenin pathway is involved in multiple stages of heart development, from the formation of the cardiac mesoderm to the differentiation of cardiac cells and the patterning of the heart. Proper regulation of Wnt signaling is essential for heart morphogenesis, and both excessive and insufficient Wnt activity can lead to congenital heart defects.

4.2.4 Liver and Pancreas Development

Wnt/β-Catenin signaling is also crucial for the development of endodermal organs such as the liver and pancreas. The pathway regulates the proliferation and differentiation of progenitor cells into hepatocytes and pancreatic cells, respectively. In liver development, Wnt signaling helps establish liver-specific gene expression patterns, while in the pancreas, it controls the balance between endocrine and exocrine cell lineages.

4.2.5 Skin and Hair Follicle Development

The development of the skin and hair follicles is another process governed by Wnt/β-Catenin signaling. The pathway is critical for the initiation of hair follicle formation and the regulation of hair cycle phases. Wnt signaling interacts with other pathways, such as BMP and Hedgehog signaling, to ensure the proper patterning and growth of skin appendages.

4.3 Cell Fate Determination

Cell fate determination refers to the process by which cells are directed to differentiate into specific cell types. The Wnt/β-Catenin pathway plays a key role in this process by regulating the expression of genes that control cell identity and differentiation.

4.3.1 Stem Cell Maintenance and Differentiation

Wnt/β-Catenin signaling is essential for maintaining the balance between stem cell renewal and differentiation. In stem cell niches, such as the intestinal crypts and the hair follicle bulge, Wnt signaling maintains the pool of undifferentiated stem cells. When Wnt signaling is reduced or inhibited, stem cells are more likely to differentiate into specific cell lineages, such as enterocytes in the intestine or keratinocytes in the skin.

4.3.2 Hematopoiesis

Wnt signaling is involved in the regulation of hematopoietic stem cells (HSCs) in the bone marrow, influencing their self-renewal and differentiation into various blood cell lineages. The pathway plays a role in the early stages of hematopoiesis, where it helps to maintain the pluripotency of HSCs. Dysregulation of Wnt signaling in HSCs can lead to hematological disorders, including leukemias.

4.3.3 Mesodermal and Endodermal Differentiation

During early embryogenesis, Wnt/β-Catenin signaling influences the differentiation of mesodermal and endodermal cells, guiding the formation of tissues such as muscle, bone, and the gut. The pathway interacts with other signaling pathways, such as TGF-β and FGF, to coordinate the differentiation of progenitor cells into specific mesodermal and endodermal lineages.

4.3.4 Neural Crest Cell Differentiation

Neural crest cells are multipotent progenitor cells that give rise to a diverse range of cell types, including neurons, glial cells, melanocytes, and craniofacial cartilage. Wnt/β-Catenin signaling is crucial for the induction and migration of neural crest cells, as well as their differentiation into various derivatives. The pathway ensures that neural crest cells migrate to their correct locations and differentiate according to their final destinations.

4.3.5 Implications in Regenerative Medicine

Understanding the role of Wnt/β-Catenin signaling in cell fate determination has significant implications for regenerative medicine. By modulating Wnt signaling, it may be possible to direct stem cell differentiation in vitro for tissue engineering and cell-based therapies. In addition, targeting Wnt signaling pathways offers potential strategies for enhancing tissue regeneration and repair in vivo, particularly in contexts such as wound healing and organ regeneration.

Conclusion

The Wnt/β-Catenin signaling pathway is integral to the orchestration of embryogenesis, influencing axis formation, organogenesis, tissue patterning, and cell fate determination. Its ability to regulate these fundamental processes highlights its importance in both normal development and the potential for therapeutic intervention in developmental disorders and regenerative medicine. This chapter underscores the breadth of Wnt/β-Catenin's influence on embryonic development, providing a foundation for understanding its broader roles in physiology and disease.

CHAPTER FIVE

Wnt Signaling in Tissue Homeostasis

Wnt signaling, particularly the Wnt/β-Catenin pathway, is essential for maintaining tissue homeostasis throughout an organism's life. This chapter delves into the roles of Wnt signaling in the maintenance of stem cell populations, its involvement in adult tissue renewal, and its specific functions in the gastrointestinal tract, skin, and hair follicle biology.

5.1 Maintenance of Stem Cell Populations

Stem cells are undifferentiated cells with the capacity for self-renewal and differentiation into various cell types. The Wnt/β-Catenin pathway is a critical regulator of stem cell maintenance across multiple tissues.

5.1.1 Wnt Signaling in Stem Cell Niches

Stem cell niches are specialized microenvironments that regulate the behavior of stem cells, including their proliferation, differentiation, and quiescence. Wnt signaling plays a pivotal role in these niches, ensuring that stem cells remain undifferentiated and retain their ability to self-renew. In the intestinal crypts, for example, Wnt/β-Catenin signaling is required to maintain the pool of intestinal stem cells (ISCs) located at the base of the crypt. These cells are responsible for the continuous renewal of the intestinal epithelium.

5.1.2 Balance Between Self-Renewal and Differentiation

The Wnt pathway helps to balance stem cell self-renewal and differentiation. High levels of Wnt signaling generally promote self-renewal and proliferation, while reduced Wnt activity can trigger differentiation. In hematopoiesis, Wnt signaling maintains the pluripotency of hematopoietic stem cells (HSCs), allowing them to generate all blood cell types. Dysregulation of Wnt signaling in this context can lead to impaired blood cell production or leukemias.

5.1.2 Wnt Signaling and Aging

The activity of Wnt signaling in stem cells is also linked to the aging process. As organisms age, changes in Wnt signaling can affect stem cell function, leading to reduced regenerative capacity and the onset of age-related diseases. In some tissues, hyperactivation of Wnt signaling has been associated with stem cell exhaustion, whereas in others, diminished Wnt activity contributes to the decline in stem cell numbers and function.

5.2 Role in Adult Tissue Renewal

Wnt/β-Catenin signaling is not only critical for embryonic development but also plays an essential role in the renewal and repair of adult tissues.

5.2.1 Epithelial Tissue Renewal

Epithelial tissues, such as those lining the gastrointestinal tract and skin, undergo constant turnover, requiring a steady supply of new cells from stem cells. Wnt signaling is crucial in driving the proliferation of progenitor cells that replace aged or damaged epithelial cells. In the skin, Wnt signaling promotes the proliferation of basal keratinocytes, which are essential for skin renewal and wound healing. Similarly, in the intestinal epithelium, Wnt/β-Catenin signaling maintains the high proliferative activity of ISCs.

5.2.2 Bone and Muscle Regeneration

Wnt signaling also plays a significant role in the regeneration of bone and muscle tissues. In bone, Wnt/β-Catenin is involved in the differentiation of osteoblasts, the cells responsible for bone formation. Wnt signaling influences muscle regeneration by regulating the activity of satellite cells, the muscle stem cells that repair and regenerate muscle tissue following injury. Dysregulation of Wnt signaling in muscle can lead to impaired muscle regeneration and muscle-wasting conditions.

5.2.3 Wnt Signaling in Liver and Lung Repair

The liver has a remarkable ability to regenerate after injury, and Wnt signaling is a key regulator of this process. It controls the proliferation and differentiation of hepatocytes during liver regeneration. In the lungs, Wnt signaling is involved in the repair of the alveolar epithelium following injury. It regulates the balance between the proliferation of progenitor cells and their differentiation into specialized lung cells.

5.2.4 Impact on Cancer

While Wnt signaling is essential for tissue renewal, its dysregulation can contribute to the development of cancer. In many cancers, including colorectal, breast, and liver cancers, aberrant Wnt/β-Catenin signaling leads to uncontrolled cell proliferation and tumor growth. Understanding how Wnt signaling drives tissue renewal provides insights into cancer biology and offers potential therapeutic targets for treating Wnt-driven cancers.

5.3 Wnt/β-Catenin in the Gastrointestinal Tract, Skin, and Hair Follicle Biology

The Wnt/β-Catenin pathway plays distinct and critical roles in the maintenance and function of various tissues, particularly in the gastrointestinal tract, skin, and hair follicles.

5.3.1 Gastrointestinal Tract

The intestinal epithelium is one of the most rapidly renewing tissues in the body, with cells turning over every few days. This renewal is driven by ISCs located at the base of the crypts, which are regulated by Wnt/β-Catenin signaling. Wnt signaling maintains the undifferentiated state of ISCs and drives their proliferation. As cells migrate up the crypt-villus axis, decreasing Wnt signaling allows them to differentiate into various intestinal cell types, such as enterocytes, goblet cells, and Paneth cells. Dysregulation of Wnt signaling in the gastrointestinal tract can lead to disorders such as colorectal cancer, where mutations in the APC gene or other components of the Wnt pathway result in constitutive Wnt/β-Catenin activity.

5.3.2 Skin Biology

In the skin, Wnt/β-Catenin signaling is critical for maintaining the balance between epidermal stem cell renewal and differentiation. It controls the proliferation of basal keratinocytes and their differentiation into the various layers of the epidermis. Wnt signaling is also involved in wound healing, where it promotes the proliferation of keratinocytes and fibroblasts to repair damaged skin tissue. In chronic wounds or skin diseases like psoriasis, aberrant Wnt signaling can disrupt normal skin homeostasis.

5.3.3 Hair Follicle Biology

The hair follicle undergoes cyclical phases of growth (anagen), regression (catagen), and rest (telogen). Wnt/β-Catenin signaling is essential for initiating and maintaining the anagen phase, driving the proliferation of hair follicle stem cells and their differentiation into hair-producing cells. During the telogen phase, reduced Wnt signaling allows hair follicles to remain quiescent. The reactivation of Wnt signaling is necessary for the transition back to the anagen phase and the initiation of new hair growth. Disruptions in Wnt/β-Catenin signaling can lead to hair loss conditions such as alopecia, while overactivation of the pathway is associated with conditions like pilomatricoma, a benign tumor of hair follicle origin.

Conclusion

Wnt/β-Catenin signaling is a cornerstone of tissue homeostasis, playing a critical role in maintaining stem cell populations, supporting adult tissue renewal, and regulating specific biological processes in the gastrointestinal tract, skin, and hair follicles. Understanding the intricate balance of Wnt signaling in these contexts not only highlights its importance in normal physiology but also underscores its relevance in diseases where this balance is disrupted. This chapter provides a comprehensive overview of the role of Wnt/β-Catenin signaling in tissue homeostasis, setting the stage for further exploration of its therapeutic potential.

CHAPTER SIX

Wnt/β-Catenin and Cancer

The Wnt/β-Catenin signaling pathway is intricately involved in various aspects of cell growth, differentiation, and tissue homeostasis. Dysregulation of this pathway can lead to oncogenesis and cancer progression. This chapter explores the mechanisms through which Wnt/β-Catenin signaling becomes dysregulated in cancer, examines specific cancers associated with this pathway, and discusses therapeutic strategies targeting Wnt/β-Catenin signaling in oncology.

6.1 Mechanisms of Pathway Dysregulation in Cancer

Dysregulation of Wnt/β-Catenin signaling in cancer can occur through various mechanisms, leading to aberrant pathway activation and contributing to tumorigenesis.

6.1.1 Genetic Mutations

6.1.1.1 APC Mutations

In many cancers, particularly colorectal cancer (CRC), mutations in the adenomatous polyposis coli (APC) gene lead to loss of function of the APC protein. This mutation impairs the ability of the APC complex to degrade β-Catenin, resulting in its accumulation and activation of Wnt target genes.

6.1.1.2 CTNNB1 Mutations

Mutations in the CTNNB1 gene, which encodes β-Catenin, can lead to constitutive activation of the Wnt pathway. These mutations often prevent β-Catenin from being phosphorylated and degraded, leading to its accumulation in the nucleus and continuous activation of Wnt target genes.

6.1.1.3 AXIN Mutations

Mutations in AXIN, a component of the β-Catenin destruction complex, can also contribute to pathway dysregulation. These mutations disrupt the function of the destruction complex, leading to increased β-Catenin levels and pathway activation.

6.1.2 Aberrant Activation of Wnt Ligands and Receptors

6.1.2.1 Overexpression of Wnt Ligands

Overexpression of Wnt ligands, such as Wnt1 or Wnt3a, can lead to excessive activation of the Wnt pathway. This overproduction of Wnt ligands can result from genetic alterations, epigenetic changes, or aberrant signaling from surrounding cells.

6.1.2.2 Frizzled Receptor Overexpression

Overexpression or amplification of Frizzled receptors, which bind Wnt ligands, can enhance Wnt signaling. This increased receptor expression can lead to prolonged activation of the pathway even in the absence of Wnt ligands.

6.1.2.3 LRP5/6 Mutations

Mutations in the low-density lipoprotein receptor-related protein 5 (LRP5) or 6 (LRP6), which act as co-receptors in the Wnt pathway, can lead to pathway activation. These mutations may enhance Wnt signaling by increasing receptor activity or stability.

6.1.3 Dysregulation of Downstream Pathway Components

6.1.3.1 Disruption of Destruction Complex

Alterations in components of the β-Catenin destruction complex (e.g., APC, Axin, GSK-3β) can lead to decreased β-Catenin degradation. This dysregulation allows β-Catenin to accumulate and translocate to the nucleus, where it activates Wnt target genes.

6.1.3.2 Inhibitory Protein Loss

Loss or downregulation of inhibitory proteins such as Dickkopf (DKK1) or Secreted Frizzled-Related Protein (sFRP) can enhance Wnt signaling. These proteins normally inhibit Wnt signaling by binding to Wnt ligands or receptors, and their loss removes this regulatory check.

6.1.4 Epigenetic Modifications

6.1.4.1 DNA Methylation

Aberrant DNA methylation can silence genes that regulate Wnt signaling, such as APC, leading to pathway activation. Conversely, hypermethylation of Wnt antagonists can lead to loss of their expression and increased pathway activity.

6.1.4.2 Histone Modifications

Changes in histone modifications can alter the expression of Wnt pathway components or Wnt target genes. For instance, modifications that lead to a more open chromatin structure can facilitate the activation of oncogenes involved in Wnt signaling.

6.1.5 MicroRNAs

6.1.5.1 Regulation by MicroRNAs

MicroRNAs (miRNAs) can regulate Wnt/β-Catenin signaling by targeting components of the pathway for degradation or inhibiting their translation. Dysregulation of miRNAs can lead to aberrant Wnt signaling and contribute to cancer progression.

6.2 Specific Cancers Associated with Wnt/β-Catenin

Wnt/β-Catenin pathway dysregulation is implicated in various cancers, with each type exhibiting unique patterns of pathway involvement.

6.2.1 Colorectal Cancer (CRC)

6.2.1.1 APC Mutations

CRC is one of the most well-studied cancers associated with Wnt/β-Catenin signaling. Mutations in the APC gene are a hallmark of early-stage CRC, leading to unregulated β-Catenin activity and tumorigenesis.

6.2.1.2 β-Catenin Mutations

In addition to APC mutations, mutations in β-Catenin itself can drive CRC. These mutations typically occur in the phosphorylation sites of β-Catenin, preventing its degradation and leading to continuous activation of Wnt target genes.

6.2.1.3 Role of the Tumor Microenvironment

The tumor microenvironment can influence Wnt signaling in CRC, with factors such as inflammatory cytokines and growth factors modulating pathway activity.

6.2.2 Breast Cancer

6.2.2.1 β-Catenin Mutations

Mutations in β-Catenin have been identified in some breast cancers, leading to aberrant pathway activation and contributing to tumor progression.

6.2.2.2 Wnt Ligand Overexpression

Overexpression of Wnt ligands, such as Wnt1 or Wnt5a, has been observed in breast cancer and is associated with aggressive tumor behavior and poor prognosis.

6.2.2.3 Impact on Metastasis

Wnt signaling can influence breast cancer metastasis by affecting cell adhesion and motility. Elevated Wnt activity can promote epithelial-to-mesenchymal transition (EMT), a process crucial for metastasis.

6.2.3 Liver Cancer (Hepatocellular Carcinoma, HCC)

6.2.3.1 APC and β-Catenin Mutations:

Mutations in APC and β-Catenin are common in HCC and contribute to tumor development by disrupting normal liver cell function and growth regulation.

6.2.3.2 Wnt Signaling and Liver Fibrosis:

Chronic liver injury and fibrosis can enhance Wnt signaling, promoting the progression from fibrosis to HCC. Activated Wnt signaling can drive the proliferation of hepatocytes and cancer stem cells in the liver.

6.2.4 Other Cancers

6.2.4.1 Ovarian Cancer

Wnt signaling dysregulation is observed in ovarian cancer, with altered expression of Wnt ligands and receptors contributing to tumorigenesis.

6.2.4.2 Pancreatic Cancer

Wnt/β-Catenin signaling is involved in the development of pancreatic ductal adenocarcinoma (PDAC), with mutations in pathway components contributing to tumor progression.

6.2.4.3 Head and Neck Cancers

Aberrant Wnt signaling is linked to head and neck squamous cell carcinoma (HNSCC), with pathway activation contributing to cancer cell proliferation and invasion.

6.3 Therapeutic Strategies Targeting Wnt/β-Catenin in Oncology

Given the role of Wnt/β-Catenin signaling in cancer, various therapeutic strategies are being explored to target this pathway and inhibit tumor growth.

6.3.1 Wnt Pathway Inhibitors

6.3.1.1 Small Molecule Inhibitors

Small molecules that target specific components of the Wnt pathway, such as β-Catenin or its transcriptional partners (e.g., TCF/LEF), are being developed. These inhibitors aim to block the interaction between β-Catenin and TCF/LEF, thereby reducing the expression of Wnt target genes.

6.3.1.2 Monoclonal Antibodies

Antibodies targeting Wnt ligands (e.g., Wnt1, Wnt3a) or Frizzled receptors are being tested in preclinical and clinical trials. These antibodies can block Wnt ligand-receptor interactions and reduce pathway activation.

6.3.2 Targeting the Destruction Complex

6.3.2.1 Activating the Destruction Complex

Strategies that enhance the activity of the β-Catenin destruction complex are being explored. These approaches aim to promote the degradation of β-Catenin and inhibit its nuclear translocation.

6.3.2..2 GSK-3β Activators

Compounds that activate glycogen synthase kinase-3β (GSK-3β) could help restore its function in the destruction complex, leading to increased degradation of β-Catenin.

6.3.3 Targeting Wnt/β-Catenin Interactions

6.3.3.1 β-Catenin-Transcription Factor Inhibitors

Inhibitors that specifically disrupt the interaction between β-Catenin and TCF/LEF transcription factors are being developed. These inhibitors aim to prevent the transcription of Wnt target genes involved in cancer progression.

6.3.4 Modulating the Tumor Microenvironment

6.3.4.1 Inhibiting Wnt Ligand Overexpression

Therapies targeting the overproduction of Wnt ligands or their release into the tumor microenvironment are being investigated. These approaches aim to reduce the overall Wnt signaling activity in the tumor.

6.3.4.2 Immune Modulation

Immunotherapies that target the Wnt pathway or modulate immune responses in the tumor microenvironment are being explored as potential treatments for Wnt-driven cancers.

6.3.5 Combining Wnt Inhibitors with Other Therapies

Combining Wnt pathway inhibitors with other cancer treatments, such as chemotherapy, targeted therapy, or immunotherapy, may enhance therapeutic efficacy and overcome resistance.

6.3.6 Personalized Medicine

6.3.6.1 Patient Stratification

Identifying patients with specific Wnt pathway mutations or dysregulations can help tailor therapies to individual tumor profiles, improving treatment outcomes and reducing adverse effects.

Conclusion

The Wnt/β-Catenin signaling pathway plays a crucial role in cancer development and progression through various mechanisms of dysregulation. Understanding the specific alterations in Wnt signaling associated with different cancers provides valuable insights for developing targeted therapies. Ongoing research into therapeutic strategies aimed at modulating Wnt signaling holds promise for advancing cancer treatment and improving patient outcomes. This chapter underscores the importance of continued investigation into Wnt/β-Catenin signaling in oncology and the development of novel therapies targeting this pivotal pathway.

CHAPTER SEVEN

Wnt/β-Catenin in Metabolic Disorders

Wnt/β-Catenin signaling is integral to many physiological processes, including development and tissue homeostasis. Emerging research highlights its significant role in metabolic disorders such as obesity and diabetes. This chapter explores the connection between Wnt signaling and these metabolic conditions, emphasizing its involvement in adipogenesis and lipid metabolism.

7.1 Connection Between Wnt Signaling and Obesity, Diabetes

Wnt/β-Catenin signaling has been implicated in the regulation of metabolic processes and has been shown to influence the development of obesity and type 2 diabetes. The pathway affects various metabolic pathways and cellular functions, linking it to these prevalent disorders

7.1.1 Obesity

7.1.1.1 Role in Adipocyte Differentiation

Wnt signaling is crucial in regulating the differentiation of pre-adipocytes into mature adipocytes. Disruption of Wnt signaling pathways can lead to an imbalance in adipocyte differentiation and function, contributing to obesity.

7.1.1.2 Wnt/β-Catenin Signaling in White and Brown Adipose Tissue

7.1.1.2.1 White Adipose Tissue

In white adipose tissue, excessive activation of Wnt/β-Catenin signaling has been associated with impaired adipogenesis and increased fat accumulation. Aberrant Wnt signaling can lead to the accumulation of dysfunctional adipocytes, promoting obesity.

7.1.1.2.2 Brown Adipose Tissue

In contrast, Wnt signaling influences the differentiation of brown adipocytes, which are involved in thermogenesis. Reduced Wnt signaling in brown adipose tissue can impair thermogenic capacity, contributing to the development of obesity.

7.1.2 Type 2 Diabetes

7.1.2.1 Insulin Resistance

Dysregulation of Wnt/β-Catenin signaling can affect insulin sensitivity and glucose metabolism. Increased Wnt signaling in insulin-sensitive tissues can lead to insulin resistance, a hallmark of type 2 diabetes.

7.1.2.2 Pancreatic β-Cell Function

Wnt signaling impacts the function and survival of pancreatic β-cells, which are responsible for insulin production. Altered Wnt signaling can impair β-cell function and contribute to the development of diabetes.

7.1.2.3 Liver Metabolism

In the liver, Wnt signaling affects glucose and lipid metabolism. Dysregulation of Wnt/β-Catenin signaling can lead to hepatic insulin resistance and dyslipidemia, exacerbating type 2 diabetes.

7.2 Role in Adipogenesis and Lipid Metabolism

Wnt/β-Catenin signaling is a key regulator of adipogenesis and lipid metabolism, influencing the development and function of adipose tissue.

7.2.1 Adipogenesis

7.2.1.1 Regulation of Pre-Adipocyte Differentiation

Wnt signaling regulates the differentiation of pre-adipocytes into mature adipocytes. Inhibition of Wnt signaling is typically required for the proper differentiation and maturation of adipocytes. Wnt/β-Catenin signaling antagonizes adipogenesis by inhibiting key transcription factors like PPARγ (peroxisome proliferator-activated receptor gamma) and C/EBPα (CCAAT/enhancer-binding protein alpha), which are essential for adipocyte differentiation.

7.2.1.2 Impact of Wnt Inhibitors

Factors that inhibit Wnt signaling, such as Wnt antagonists (e.g., Dickkopf-1, sFRP), can promote adipocyte differentiation and increase fat accumulation. Overexpression of these antagonists has been linked to obesity and metabolic dysfunction.

7.2.1.3 Effect on White and Brown Adipocytes

Wnt signaling influences both white and brown adipogenesis. While high Wnt activity generally inhibits white adipocyte differentiation, it may promote brown adipocyte formation under certain conditions, contributing to variations in fat storage and energy expenditure.

7.2.2 Lipid Metabolism

7.2.2.1 Regulation of Lipid Synthesis and Storage

Wnt signaling impacts lipid synthesis and storage in adipocytes. β-Catenin activation can modulate the expression of genes involved in lipid metabolism, such as those encoding fatty acid synthase and lipoprotein lipase.

7.2.2.2 Fatty Acid Oxidation

Wnt signaling also affects fatty acid oxidation and mitochondrial function. Altered Wnt signaling can disrupt normal fatty acid oxidation processes, leading to lipid accumulation and metabolic disorders.

7.2.2.3 Interaction with Other Pathways

Wnt/β-Catenin signaling interacts with other metabolic pathways, such as those involving AMPK (AMP-activated protein kinase) and mTOR (mechanistic target of rapamycin). These interactions can influence overall lipid metabolism and energy balance.

7.2.3 Metabolic Syndrome

7.2.3.1 Integration with Metabolic Syndrome

The interplay between Wnt/β-Catenin signaling and metabolic syndrome components, such as hypertension, dyslipidemia, and insulin resistance, is an area of active research. Dysregulation of Wnt signaling can exacerbate these conditions, leading to a higher risk of cardiovascular disease and other complications.

7.3 Therapeutic Implications

Understanding the role of Wnt/β-Catenin signaling in metabolic disorders offers potential therapeutic avenues for managing obesity and diabetes.

7.3.1 Targeting Wnt Pathway Components

7.3.1.1 Wnt Inhibitors

Developing small molecule inhibitors or antibodies targeting specific components of the Wnt pathway may help modulate its activity and address metabolic disorders. These inhibitors could potentially reduce excessive Wnt signaling that contributes to obesity or insulin resistance.

7.3.1.2 Wnt Agonists

In some cases, activating Wnt signaling may be beneficial, such as enhancing the differentiation of brown adipocytes or improving insulin sensitivity. Identifying compounds that can selectively activate Wnt signaling in specific tissues may provide therapeutic benefits.

7.3.2 Lifestyle and Dietary Interventions

7.3.2.1 Modulation of Wnt Signaling through Diet

Nutritional interventions and dietary components can influence Wnt signaling. For example, certain polyphenols and bioactive compounds may modulate Wnt signaling and impact metabolic health.

7.3.2.2 Exercise and Wnt Signaling

Regular physical activity can influence Wnt signaling pathways and improve metabolic health. Exercise-induced changes in Wnt signaling may contribute to better adipose tissue function and glucose metabolism.

7.3.3 Personalized Approaches:

7.3.3.1 Genetic and Molecular Profiling

Personalized medicine approaches that assess genetic and molecular profiles related to Wnt signaling can help tailor interventions and treatments for individuals with metabolic disorders. Identifying specific mutations or dysregulations in Wnt signaling pathways may guide targeted therapies.

Conclusion

Wnt/β-Catenin signaling plays a crucial role in metabolic disorders such as obesity and type 2 diabetes by regulating adipogenesis and lipid metabolism. Dysregulation of this pathway can lead to impaired metabolic function and contribute to the development of these prevalent conditions. Understanding the mechanisms through which Wnt signaling influences metabolic processes provides insights into potential therapeutic strategies and interventions. Continued research into Wnt/β-Catenin signaling and its impact on metabolic health is essential for developing effective treatments and improving management of metabolic disorders.

CHAPTER EIGHT

Wnt/β-Catenin in Neurodegenerative Diseases

The Wnt/β-Catenin signaling pathway is critical for various aspects of neuronal development, maintenance, and function. Dysregulation of this pathway has been implicated in several neurodegenerative diseases, including Alzheimer's disease (AD), Parkinson's disease (PD), and other conditions. This chapter provides a comprehensive overview of the role of Wnt/β-Catenin signaling in neuronal health and its involvement in neurodegenerative disorders.

8.1 Wnt/β-Catenin in Neuronal Development and Maintenance

Wnt/β-Catenin signaling is crucial for neuronal development, plasticity, and maintenance. This pathway influences several key processes in the central nervous system (CNS).

8.1.1 Neuronal Development

8.1.1.1 Neurogenesis

During development, Wnt/β-Catenin signaling regulates neurogenesis by controlling the proliferation and differentiation of neural progenitor cells. Wnt signaling influences the fate of neural stem cells, directing their differentiation into various neuronal subtypes.

8.1.1.2 Neuronal Migration

Proper neuronal migration, which is essential for correct brain wiring, is regulated by Wnt signaling. Wnt/β-Catenin signaling affects the cytoskeletal dynamics and cellular adhesion necessary for neuronal migration.

8.1.1.3 Synaptic Formation and Plasticity

Wnt signaling plays a role in synaptogenesis and the modulation of synaptic plasticity. It regulates the formation and maintenance of synaptic connections, which are critical for learning and memory processes.

8.1.2 Neuronal Maintenance

8.1.2.1 Cell Survival and Protection

Wnt/β-Catenin signaling contributes to neuronal survival by promoting cell-protective mechanisms and preventing apoptosis. It regulates the expression of neuroprotective factors and anti-apoptotic genes.

8.1.2.2 Neuroinflammation Modulation

The pathway modulates neuroinflammation, which is important for maintaining a healthy neuronal environment. Dysregulation of Wnt signaling can lead to increased neuroinflammation and neuronal damage.

8.1.3 Neurodegeneration and Repair

8.1.3.1 Neuroprotection

Wnt/β-Catenin signaling has neuroprotective effects, and its activation has been shown to protect neurons from various stressors and toxins. This protective role is significant in the context of neurodegenerative diseases.

8.1.3.2 Neuronal Repair

The pathway is involved in neurorepair processes, including the regeneration of damaged neurons and the promotion of neurogenesis in response to injury or disease.

8.2 Pathway's Role in Alzheimer's, Parkinson's, and Other Neurodegenerative Conditions

Wnt/β-Catenin signaling dysregulation is implicated in the pathogenesis of various neurodegenerative diseases. Understanding its role in these conditions provides insights into potential therapeutic strategies.

8.2.1 Alzheimer's Disease (AD)

8.2.1.1 Amyloid-β and Tau Pathology

Abnormalities in Wnt/β-Catenin signaling are associated with amyloid-β (Aβ) plaque formation and tau hyperphosphorylation, key features of AD. Wnt signaling can influence the processing of amyloid precursor protein (APP) and the accumulation of Aβ.

8.2.1.2 Cognitive Decline

Impaired Wnt signaling has been linked to cognitive decline in AD. Wnt signaling is involved in synaptic plasticity and memory formation, and its disruption can contribute to cognitive impairments observed in AD patients.

8.2.1.3 Neuroinflammation

Dysregulation of Wnt/β-Catenin signaling can exacerbate neuroinflammation in AD. Chronic inflammation and activation of microglia contribute to neuronal damage and disease progression.

8.2.2 Parkinson's Disease (PD)

8.2.2.1 Dopaminergic Neuron Degeneration

In PD, Wnt/β-Catenin signaling is implicated in the degeneration of dopaminergic neurons in the substantia nigra. Dysregulation of the pathway affects neuronal survival and function, contributing to the loss of dopaminergic neurons.

8.2.2.2 α-Synuclein Aggregation

Wnt signaling influences the aggregation and clearance of α-synuclein, a protein associated with PD. Abnormal Wnt signaling may affect the accumulation and toxicity of α-synuclein aggregates.

8.2.2.3 Motor Dysfunction

Impaired Wnt signaling can contribute to motor dysfunction observed in PD. The pathway's role in dopaminergic neuron function and neuroprotection is critical for maintaining motor control.

8.2.3 Other Neurodegenerative Conditions

8.2.3.1 Huntington's Disease (HD)

In HD, Wnt/β-Catenin signaling is disrupted, affecting neuronal survival and function. The pathway's dysregulation may contribute to the progressive neurodegeneration and motor symptoms characteristic of HD.

8.2.3.3 Amyotrophic Lateral Sclerosis (ALS)

Wnt signaling abnormalities have been observed in ALS, where the pathway's dysregulation may affect motor neuron function and survival. Research into Wnt signaling in ALS aims to understand its impact on disease progression and motor neuron loss.

8.2.3.3 Multiple Sclerosis (MS)

Wnt/β-Catenin signaling may influence the inflammatory and demyelinating processes in MS. The pathway's role in regulating immune responses and neuroinflammation is relevant for understanding MS pathology and potential therapeutic interventions.

8.3 Therapeutic Implications

Given the involvement of Wnt/β-Catenin signaling in neurodegenerative diseases, targeting this pathway offers potential therapeutic strategies.

8.3.1 Modulating Wnt Signaling

8.3.1.1 Wnt Agonists

Small molecules or biologics that activate Wnt/β-Catenin signaling may provide neuroprotective effects and promote neuronal survival. These agents could enhance synaptic plasticity and cognitive function in neurodegenerative diseases.

8.3.1.2 Wnt Inhibitors

In conditions where Wnt signaling is excessively activated, inhibitors that block the pathway may help reduce pathological features, such as amyloid-β deposition or α-synuclein aggregation.

8.3.2 Targeting Specific Pathway Components

8.3.2.1 β-Catenin Stabilizers

Agents that stabilize β-Catenin and enhance its activity in the nucleus may be beneficial for neuroprotection and repair. Targeting β-Catenin stabilization can promote the expression of neuroprotective genes and improve neuronal function.

8.3.2.2 Modulating Destruction Complex

Compounds that influence the β-Catenin destruction complex (e.g., APC, Axin, GSK-3β) could be used to adjust pathway activity and address its dysregulation in neurodegenerative diseases.

8.3.3 Gene Therapy and Cellular Approaches

8.3.3.1 Gene Editing

Techniques such as CRISPR/Cas9 could be used to correct genetic mutations or dysregulations in Wnt signaling components, offering a potential strategy for disease modification.

8.3.3.2 Cell Therapy

Stem cell-based therapies that utilize Wnt signaling to enhance neuronal differentiation and integration may offer potential treatments for neurodegenerative conditions.

8.3.4 Lifestyle and Dietary Interventions

8.3.4.1 Nutritional Modulation

Dietary components that influence Wnt signaling, such as polyphenols and other bioactive compounds, may have neuroprotective effects and support brain health.

8.3.4.2 Exercise

Physical activity has been shown to impact Wnt signaling and promote neurogenesis, offering potential benefits for individuals with neurodegenerative diseases.

Conclusion

Wnt/β-Catenin signaling plays a pivotal role in neuronal development, maintenance, and neuroprotection. Dysregulation of this pathway is associated with various neurodegenerative diseases, including Alzheimer's and Parkinson's diseases, and may contribute to disease progression through mechanisms such as impaired neuronal survival, inflammation, and protein aggregation. Targeting Wnt/β-Catenin signaling offers potential therapeutic avenues for treating neurodegenerative conditions and improving neuronal health. Continued research into the role of Wnt signaling in neurodegenerative diseases is essential for developing effective treatments and understanding the complexities of these disorders.

CHAPTER NINE

Wnt/β-Catenin and Bone Health

The Wnt/β-Catenin signaling pathway is a critical regulator of bone health, influencing processes such as osteogenesis, bone remodeling, and the pathogenesis of bone diseases. This chapter delves into the role of Wnt/β-Catenin signaling in maintaining bone health and its involvement in bone-related conditions like osteoporosis and other bone diaseases.

9.1 Osteogenesis and Bone Remodeling

Wnt/β-Catenin signaling is fundamental to osteogenesis (bone formation) and bone remodeling (the ongoing process of bone resorption and formation). Its regulation of these processes impacts overall bone health and skeletal integrity.

9.1.1 Osteogenesis

9.1.1.1 Osteoblast Differentiation

Wnt/β-Catenin signaling is essential for the differentiation of mesenchymal stem cells (MSCs) into osteoblasts, the cells responsible for bone formation. Activation of Wnt signaling promotes the expression of key osteogenic transcription factors, such as Runx2 (runt-related transcription factor 2) and Osterix (Osx), which drive the development and maturation of osteoblasts.

9.1.1.2 Bone Matrix Formation

Osteoblasts produce the bone matrix, including collagen and mineralized components. Wnt signaling enhances the synthesis of extracellular matrix proteins, contributing to bone matrix formation and mineralization.

9.1.2 Bone Remodeling:

9.1.2.1 Balance Between Osteoblasts and Osteoclasts

Bone remodeling involves the coordinated activity of osteoblasts (bone-forming cells) and osteoclasts (bone-resorbing cells). Wnt/β-Catenin signaling influences the balance between these cell types. Activation of Wnt signaling in osteoblasts promotes bone formation, while it also regulates the RANKL/OPG (receptor activator of nuclear factor kappa-B ligand/osteoprotegerin) pathway to modulate osteoclastogenesis and bone resorption.

9.1.2.2 Bone Resorption

In addition to promoting osteoblast differentiation, Wnt signaling affects the activity of osteoclasts indirectly. Wnt signaling can influence the production of RANKL by osteoblasts, which in turn stimulates osteoclast differentiation and activity. Proper regulation ensures that bone resorption and formation are balanced to maintain bone homeostasis.

9.1.2.3 Bone Quality and Strength

Beyond bone quantity, Wnt/β-Catenin signaling also impacts bone quality and strength. It affects bone density, trabecular architecture, and mechanical properties, which are crucial for preventing fractures and maintaining overall skeletal health.

9.2 Wnt Signaling in Osteoporosis and Other Bone Diseases

Dysregulation of Wnt/β-Catenin signaling is implicated in various bone diseases, including osteoporosis and other conditions affecting bone health. Understanding these alterations helps in developing targeted therapies.

9.2.1 Osteoporosis

9.2.1.1 Pathogenesis

Osteoporosis is characterized by reduced bone density and increased fracture risk due to an imbalance between bone resorption and formation. Wnt/β-Catenin signaling plays a crucial role in this process. In osteoporosis, there is often decreased Wnt signaling activity, leading to reduced osteoblast differentiation and bone formation.

9.2.1.2 Role of Wnt Inhibitors

Increased levels of Wnt antagonists, such as sFRP (secreted frizzled-related protein) and Dkk1 (Dickkopf-1), can inhibit Wnt signaling and contribute to bone loss. These inhibitors interfere with the Wnt pathway, impairing osteoblast function and promoting osteoporosis.

9.2.1.3 Therapeutic Strategies

Targeting Wnt signaling to enhance osteoblast activity and bone formation is a potential therapeutic approach for osteoporosis. Agents that inhibit Wnt antagonists or activate Wnt signaling could help improve bone density and reduce fracture risk.

9.2.2 Other Bone Diseases

9.2.2.1 Paget's Disease

Paget's disease is characterized by abnormal bone remodeling, leading to enlarged and weakened bones. Wnt/β-Catenin signaling is involved in regulating osteoclast activity and bone formation, and its dysregulation may contribute to the pathological bone remodeling seen in Paget's disease.

9.2.2.2 Bone Tumors

Certain bone tumors, such as osteosarcoma, exhibit alterations in Wnt signaling pathways. Aberrant Wnt/β-Catenin signaling in these tumors can influence cell proliferation, differentiation, and metastasis. Understanding the role of Wnt signaling in bone tumors provides insights into potential therapeutic targets.

9.2.2.3 Bone Dysplasias

Genetic bone dysplasias, such as osteogenesis imperfecta, can involve mutations affecting Wnt signaling components. These conditions often result in defective bone formation and strength, highlighting the importance of Wnt signaling in normal bone development.

9.2.3 Aging and Bone Health

9.2.3.1 Age-Related Changes

Aging is associated with changes in Wnt signaling that can impact bone health. Decreased Wnt signaling activity with age may contribute to reduced bone formation and increased susceptibility to osteoporosis. Research into age-related alterations in Wnt signaling can inform strategies for preventing and treating age-related bone loss.

9.3 Therapeutic Implications

Given the role of Wnt/β-Catenin signaling in bone health, targeting this pathway offers potential therapeutic strategies for managing bone diseases.

9.3.1 Wnt Pathway Modulators

9.3.1.1 Wnt Activators

Small molecules or biologics that activate Wnt/β-Catenin signaling may promote osteoblast differentiation and bone formation. These activators can counteract the effects of Wnt antagonists and enhance bone density in conditions like osteoporosis.

9.3.1.2 Wnt Inhibitors

In diseases characterized by excessive Wnt signaling, such as certain bone tumors, inhibitors targeting the pathway may be beneficial. These inhibitors can reduce abnormal bone growth and tumor progression.

9.3.2 Bone-Anabolic Agents

9.3.2.1 Sclerostin Inhibitors

Sclerostin is a protein that inhibits Wnt/β-Catenin signaling and bone formation. Inhibitors of sclerostin, such as romosozumab, can enhance bone formation and improve bone density in patients with osteoporosis.

9.3.2.2 Anti-Resorptive Agents

Combining Wnt signaling modulators with anti-resorptive agents (e.g., bisphosphonates) may provide a comprehensive approach to treating bone diseases by addressing both bone formation and resorption.

9.3.3 Gene Therapy and Cellular Approaches

9.3.3.1 Gene Editing

Techniques like CRISPR/Cas9 could be used to correct genetic mutations affecting Wnt signaling components, offering potential treatments for genetic bone disorders.

9.3.3.2 Stem Cell Therapy

Stem cell-based approaches that utilize Wnt signaling to promote osteoblast differentiation and bone regeneration may offer novel therapies for bone diseases and fractures.

9.3.4 Lifestyle and Nutritional Interventions

9.3.4.1 Diet and Bone Health

Nutritional components that influence Wnt signaling, such as calcium and vitamin D, play a role in maintaining bone health. Dietary interventions that support Wnt signaling may help in preventing and managing bone diseases.

9.3.4.2 Exercise

Weight-bearing exercise can positively impact Wnt signaling and bone health, promoting bone formation and strength.

Conclusion

Wnt/β-Catenin signaling is a key regulator of osteogenesis and bone remodeling, affecting bone health and the pathogenesis of bone diseases. Dysregulation of this pathway contributes to conditions such as osteoporosis, Paget's disease, and bone tumors. Targeting Wnt signaling offers potential therapeutic strategies for managing these diseases and improving bone health. Continued research into the mechanisms of Wnt signaling in bone health is essential for developing effective treatments and enhancing our understanding of bone disorders.

Part III: Therapeutic Approaches and Future Directions

Chapter 10: Small Molecule Inhibitors of Wnt/β-Catenin

Provides an overview of current small molecule inhibitors targeting the Wnt/β-Catenin pathway, their mechanisms of action, and their potential in therapeutic applications.

Chapter 11: Biological Therapeutics Targeting Wnt/β-Catenin

Discusses antibodies, peptides, and other biologics designed to modulate Wnt signaling, along with gene therapy approaches and the challenges associated with these strategies.

Chapter 12: Modulation of Wnt/β-Catenin in Regenerative Medicine

Explores how Wnt/β-Catenin signaling can be harnessed to enhance tissue repair and regeneration, including applications in wound healing and organ repair.

Chapter 13: Novel Insights into Wnt/β-Catenin Signaling

Highlights recent discoveries and paradigm shifts in Wnt signaling, cross-talk with other pathways, and technological advancements in research.

Chapter 14: Future Prospects and Challenges

Looks ahead to emerging therapeutic strategies, unresolved questions in Wnt signaling research, and the potential for personalized medicine.

Chapter 15: Case Studies and Clinical Applications

Provides real-world case studies illustrating the role of Wnt/β-Catenin signaling in various diseases and the translation of basic research into clinical applications.

Chapter 16: Techniques to Study Wnt/β-Catenin Pathway

Describes the experimental techniques used to study Wnt signaling, including in vitro and in vivo models, imaging methods, molecular biology techniques, and high-throughput screening methods.

Chapter 17: Computational Modeling of Wnt/β-Catenin Signaling

Discusses computational approaches to studying Wnt signaling, including bioinformatics, systems biology models, and predictive modeling in drug discovery.

CHAPTER TEN

Small Molecule Inhibitors of Wnt/β-Catenin

Small molecule inhibitors of Wnt/β-Catenin signaling represent a promising approach for modulating the pathway's activity in various diseases. This chapter provides a comprehensive overview of current inhibitors, their mechanisms of action, and their therapeutic potential based on clinical trials.

10.1 Overview of Current Inhibitors

Small molecule inhibitors targeting the Wnt/β-Catenin pathway have been developed to modulate its activity in various pathological conditions. These inhibitors are designed to interfere with specific components of the Wnt signaling cascade to either block excessive activation or enhance pathway activity where needed.

10.1.1 Inhibitors of Wnt Ligands

10.1.1.1 ETC-159 (Establishment Therapeutics)

This small molecule inhibits Wnt signaling by targeting Wnt ligands directly. It has been shown to reduce Wnt pathway activity and is under investigation for its efficacy in various cancers.

10.1.2 Inhibitors of Frizzled Receptors

10.1.2.1 Omp-54F28 (OncoMed Pharmaceuticals)

This fusion protein combines a soluble Frizzled receptor with the Fc portion of IgG. It acts as a decoy receptor, binding to Wnt ligands and preventing their interaction with native Frizzled receptors.

10.1.2.2 FZD8-Fc

Another fusion protein that targets specific Frizzled receptors involved in Wnt signaling, blocking their interaction with Wnt ligands.

10.1.3 Inhibitors of β-Catenin

10.1.3.1 IWP-2

This compound inhibits β-Catenin by targeting its interaction with the TCF/LEF1 transcription factors. It has been shown to effectively reduce β-Catenin-dependent transcriptional activity.

10.1.3.2 XAV939

A well-known small molecule that inhibits the Wnt pathway by stabilizing Axin, a component of the β-Catenin destruction complex. This stabilization promotes the degradation of β-Catenin and reduces its nuclear accumulation.

10.1.4 Inhibitors of Destruction Complex Components

10.1.4.1 BML-284

This molecule specifically inhibits GSK-3β, a key kinase in the β-Catenin destruction complex. By inhibiting GSK-3β, BML-284 promotes β-Catenin accumulation and nuclear translocation.

10.1.4.2 PP1 (Protein Phosphatase 1)

This small molecule targets various components of the destruction complex, including CK1 and GSK-3β, to modulate β-Catenin stability.

10.1.5 Inhibitors of TCF/LEF Transcription Factors

10.1.5.1 TCF/LEF Inhibitors

Small molecules that directly target TCF/LEF1 transcription factors to prevent their interaction with β-Catenin. These inhibitors are designed to block β-Catenin-mediated transcriptional activation.

10.2 Mechanisms of Action

The small molecule inhibitors of Wnt/β-Catenin signaling act through various mechanisms to modulate the pathway's activity. Understanding these mechanisms helps in evaluating their potential effectiveness and specificity.

10.2.1 Inhibition of Wnt Ligand Binding

Inhibitors like ETC-159 prevent Wnt ligands from binding to Frizzled receptors. By sequestering Wnt ligands, these inhibitors block the initiation of Wnt signaling, preventing activation of downstream β-Catenin pathways.

10.2.2 Blocking Frizzled Receptor Activation

Fusion proteins like Omp-54F28 act as decoy receptors, binding to Wnt ligands and preventing their interaction with native Frizzled receptors. This prevents the activation of the Frizzled receptor and subsequent β-Catenin stabilization.

10.2.3 Inhibition of β-Catenin Stabilization

Inhibitors like XAV939 stabilize Axin, a component of the β-Catenin destruction complex. Stabilization of Axin promotes the degradation of β-Catenin, reducing its accumulation and nuclear translocation.

10.2.4 Inhibition of Destruction Complex Components

Compounds like BML-284 inhibit GSK-3β, preventing the phosphorylation and degradation of β-Catenin. This leads to increased β-Catenin levels and enhanced signaling, which can be beneficial in contexts requiring increased Wnt activity.

10.2.5 Targeting TCF/LEF1 Transcription Factors

Inhibitors targeting TCF/LEF1 transcription factors block their ability to bind to β-Catenin and activate target gene transcription. This prevents the downstream effects of β-Catenin-mediated transcriptional activation.

10.3 Clinical Trials and Therapeutic Potential

The therapeutic potential of small molecule inhibitors of Wnt/β-Catenin signaling is being evaluated through clinical trials, with promising results in various diseases. These trials aim to assess the safety, efficacy, and clinical benefits of these inhibitors.

10.3.1 Cancer Therapy

10.3.1.1 Colon Cancer

Inhibitors like ETC-159 are being tested in clinical trials for their efficacy in treating colorectal cancer, where Wnt/β-Catenin signaling is often dysregulated. Early results suggest potential benefits in reducing tumor growth and improving patient outcomes.

10.3.1.2 Breast Cancer

Small molecules targeting Wnt signaling are also being evaluated for breast cancer, where aberrant Wnt signaling contributes to tumor progression and metastasis. Clinical trials are assessing the effectiveness of these inhibitors in combination with other therapies.

10.3.2 Bone Disease (Osteoporosis)

Inhibitors that target excessive Wnt signaling may offer potential benefits in treating osteoporosis by promoting bone formation and improving bone density. Clinical trials are investigating the effects of these inhibitors on bone health and fracture risk.

10.3.3 Neurodegenerative Diseases

10.3.3.1 Alzheimer's and Parkinson's Diseases

Small molecules that modulate Wnt signaling are being explored for their potential to address neurodegenerative diseases. Trials are assessing their impact on disease progression, cognitive function, and neuroprotection.

10.3.4 Other Applications

10.3.4.1 Fibrotic Diseases

Wnt/β-Catenin signaling is involved in fibrosis, and inhibitors targeting this pathway may offer therapeutic benefits in conditions like liver fibrosis and pulmonary fibrosis. Clinical trials are investigating the efficacy of these inhibitors in reducing fibrosis and improving organ function.

10.3.5 Challenges and Future Directions

10.3.5.1 Specificity and Off-Target Effects

One of the challenges with Wnt inhibitors is ensuring specificity and minimizing off-target effects. Ongoing research focuses on improving the selectivity of these inhibitors to reduce potential side effects.

10.3.5.2 Combination Therapies

Combining Wnt inhibitors with other therapeutic agents may enhance efficacy and overcome resistance. Clinical trials are exploring combination strategies to improve treatment outcomes in various diseases.

Conclusion

Small molecule inhibitors of Wnt/β-Catenin signaling offer a promising approach to modulating the pathway's activity in a range of diseases. These inhibitors act through various mechanisms to either block excessive Wnt signaling or enhance pathway activity as needed. Ongoing clinical trials are assessing their safety and efficacy, with potential applications in cancer, bone diseases, neurodegenerative conditions, and other disorders. Continued research and development of these inhibitors are essential for optimizing their therapeutic potential and addressing the challenges associated with their use.

CHAPTER ELEVEN

Biological Therapeutics Targeting Wnt/β-Catenin

Biological therapeutics targeting the Wnt/β-Catenin pathway offer a promising approach to modulate this critical signaling cascade in various diseases. This chapter explores the different types of biological therapeutics, including antibodies, peptides, gene therapy approaches, and discusses the challenges and future directions in this field.

11.1 Antibodies, Peptides, and Other Biologics

Biological therapeutics targeting the Wnt/β-Catenin pathway primarily include monoclonal antibodies, peptides, and other biologics designed to modulate the pathway's activity.

11.1.1 Monoclonal Antibodies

11.1.1.1 Anti-Wnt Ligand Antibodies

These antibodies target specific Wnt ligands, preventing them from binding to Frizzled receptors. Examples include:

- **ETC-159**: A monoclonal antibody that binds to Wnt ligands, reducing their availability to Frizzled receptors and inhibiting Wnt signaling.
- **Brodalumab**: An antibody targeting Wnt3a, one of the key ligands in the Wnt/β-Catenin pathway.

11.1.1.2 Anti-Frizzled Antibodies

These antibodies target Frizzled receptors, blocking the interaction between Wnt ligands and their receptors. For example:

- **SFRP1/2 (Secreted Frizzled-Related Proteins):** These antibodies neutralize Frizzled receptors, disrupting Wnt signaling.

11.1.1.3 Anti-Dkk1 Antibodies

Dickkopf-1 (Dkk1) is a Wnt pathway antagonist. Antibodies against Dkk1, such as **Danozumab**, can inhibit its function and enhance Wnt signaling.

11.1.2 Peptides

11.1.2.1 Frizzled Peptide Inhibitors

Peptides that mimic the Wnt-binding domain of Frizzled receptors can act as competitive inhibitors, blocking Wnt ligand binding. Examples include:

- **Fzd8-CRD**: A peptide representing the cysteine-rich domain of Frizzled8 that can compete with Wnt ligands for receptor binding.

11.1.2.2 Wnt Pathway Modulator Peptides

These peptides are designed to modulate Wnt signaling by affecting various components of the pathway. For instance:

Pyrvinium: A small peptide that inhibits Wnt signaling by disrupting β-Catenin and TCF/LEF1 interactions.

11.1.3 Other Biologics

11.1.3.1 Fusion Proteins

These combine receptor extracellular domains with other proteins to inhibit Wnt signaling. Examples include:

- **Omp-54F28**: A fusion protein comprising the extracellular domain of Frizzled and the Fc domain of IgG, acting as a decoy receptor.

11.1.3.2 Small Molecule Inhibitors

Although not biologics, small molecules that target Wnt/β-Catenin signaling components (discussed in Chapter 10) are often used in conjunction with biologics for enhanced therapeutic effects.

11.2 Gene Therapy Approaches

Gene therapy approaches targeting the Wnt/β-Catenin pathway aim to modify gene expression or introduce genetic material to modulate pathway activity. These approaches can either enhance or inhibit Wnt signaling, depending on the therapeutic goal.

11.2.1 Gene Editing

11.2.1.1 CRISPR/Cas9

This technology can be used to edit genes involved in Wnt signaling, such as β-Catenin, Axin, or TCF/LEF1. By correcting mutations or introducing specific genetic changes, CRISPR/Cas9 can modulate pathway activity. Examples include:

- **Correcting Mutations**: Editing mutations in β-Catenin that lead to uncontrolled signaling in cancers.

- **Knockout Studies**: Deleting genes encoding Wnt antagonists or other signaling components to study their effects on pathway regulation.

11.2.2 Gene Silencing

11.2.2.1 RNA Interference (RNAi)

RNAi can be used to silence genes involved in Wnt signaling. This approach utilizes small interfering RNA (siRNA) or short hairpin RNA (shRNA) to reduce the expression of specific Wnt pathway components. For example:

- **Targeting β-Catenin**: Silencing β-Catenin to reduce its nuclear accumulation and transcriptional activity.
- **Inhibiting Wnt Ligands**: Using RNAi to target Wnt ligands or their receptors to reduce pathway activation.

11.2.3 Gene Augmentation

11.2.3.1 Gene Delivery

Introducing genes that encode for Wnt antagonists or pathway inhibitors into cells can modulate Wnt signaling. Examples include:

- **Introducing sFRP or Dkk1**: Delivery of genes encoding sFRP or Dkk1 to inhibit Wnt signaling in diseases where excessive activation is a problem.
- **Wnt Pathway Modulators**: Introducing genes that produce Wnt pathway modulators to either enhance or inhibit signaling depending on the disease context.

11.3 Challenges and Future Directions

Biological therapeutics targeting Wnt/β-Catenin signaling face several challenges, and future research is focused on addressing these issues to improve therapeutic outcomes.

11.3.1 Specificity and Off-Target Effects

11.3.1.1 Challenge

Ensuring specificity of biological therapeutics to avoid off-target effects and unintended modulation of other pathways is crucial. Cross-reactivity with other signaling pathways or proteins can lead to adverse effects.

11.3.1.2 Future Directions

Developing highly specific antibodies and peptides that target unique epitopes within the Wnt/β-Catenin pathway. Improved screening techniques and advanced technologies like nanobodies may enhance specificity.

11.3.2 Delivery and Bioavailability

11.3.2.1 Challenge

Efficient delivery of biologics to target tissues and cells remains a significant challenge. Issues related to stability, half-life, and delivery methods can impact the effectiveness of therapies.

11.3.2.1 Future Directions

Advancements in drug delivery systems, such as nanoparticles or liposomes, to improve the bioavailability and targeted delivery of biologics. Developing strategies for localized delivery to minimize systemic exposure.

11.3.3 Resistance and Adaptation

11.3.3.1 Challenge

Tumor cells or other disease cells may develop resistance to Wnt-targeted therapies, leading to reduced effectiveness over time.

11.3.3.2 Future Directions

Combining Wnt inhibitors with other therapeutic modalities to overcome resistance. Personalized medicine approaches to tailor therapies based on individual genetic and molecular profiles.

11.3.4 Safety and Long-Term Effects

11.3.4.1 Challenge

Long-term safety of Wnt-targeted biologics must be thoroughly evaluated to avoid potential side effects, such as unwanted activation or inhibition of Wnt signaling in normal tissues.

11.3.4.2 Future Directions

Conducting comprehensive safety assessments and long-term follow-up studies. Implementing strategies to monitor and manage potential adverse effects.

11.3.5 Regulatory and Developmental Hurdles

11.3.5.1 Challenge

Navigating regulatory requirements and developmental hurdles for approval of new biologics can be complex and time-consuming.

11.3.5.2 Future Directions

Streamlining regulatory processes and fostering collaboration between researchers, clinicians, and regulatory agencies to facilitate the development and approval of new therapies.

Conclusion

Biological therapeutics targeting the Wnt/β-Catenin pathway offer promising opportunities for modulating this critical signaling cascade in various diseases. Monoclonal antibodies, peptides, and gene therapy approaches are at the forefront of this therapeutic strategy. While challenges such as specificity, delivery, resistance, and safety need to be addressed, ongoing research and advancements in technology hold promise for overcoming these hurdles and improving therapeutic outcomes. The future of Wnt/β-Catenin-targeted therapies lies in continued innovation, improved understanding of the pathway, and collaborative efforts to bring effective treatments to clinical practice.

CHAPTER TWELVE

Modulation of Wnt/β-Catenin in Regenerative Medicine

The Wnt/β-Catenin signaling pathway plays a crucial role in tissue development, maintenance, and repair. Modulating this pathway offers significant potential in regenerative medicine, where the goal is to enhance tissue repair, regeneration, and recovery from injury or disease. This chapter explores the various strategies for modulating Wnt/β-Catenin signaling to improve regenerative outcomes, focusing on tissue repair and regeneration, applications in wound healing and organ repair, and stem cell-based therapies.

12.1 Enhancing Tissue Repair and Regeneration

Modulating the Wnt/β-Catenin pathway can accelerate tissue repair and regeneration by promoting cell proliferation, differentiation, and tissue remodeling. Various approaches are used to harness the pathway's regenerative potential.

12.1.1 Activation of Wnt Signaling

12.1.1.1 Small Molecules

Compounds that activate Wnt/β-Catenin signaling, such as **GSK-3β inhibitors** (e.g., XAV939) and **Wnt agonists** (e.g., Wnt3a), can enhance tissue repair by promoting cell proliferation and tissue growth.

12.1.1.2 Gene Therapy

Introducing genes that encode Wnt ligands or pathway components can stimulate Wnt signaling in target tissues. For example, delivering Wnt3a or β-Catenin genes to damaged tissues can boost regenerative processes.

12.1.2 Modulation of β-Catenin Activity

12.1.2.1 β-Catenin Stabilizers

Compounds that stabilize β-Catenin, preventing its degradation, can enhance regenerative responses by increasing β-Catenin levels and promoting its transcriptional activity. Examples include **Pyrvinium** and **LiCl**.

12.1.2.2 Targeted Delivery Systems

Utilizing advanced delivery systems to specifically target β-Catenin to sites of injury or disease can improve tissue repair outcomes. Nanoparticle-based delivery systems are being explored for this purpose.

12.1.3 Inhibition of Wnt Antagonists

12.1.3.1 Inhibitors of Dkk1

Blocking Wnt antagonists like Dickkopf-1 (Dkk1) can promote Wnt signaling and enhance tissue regeneration. For instance, **Danozumab**, an anti-Dkk1 antibody, is being investigated for its potential to improve regenerative outcomes in various tissues.

12.2 Applications in Wound Healing and Organ Repair

The modulation of Wnt/β-Catenin signaling holds great promise for improving wound healing and repairing damaged organs.

12.2.1 Wound Healing

12.2.1.1 Promotion of Epithelialization

Wnt signaling plays a role in epithelial cell proliferation and migration, crucial for wound closure. Modulating this pathway can accelerate epithelialization and wound healing.

- **Topical Application of Wnt Agonists:** Applying Wnt agonists or β-Catenin stabilizers directly to wound sites can enhance epithelial cell proliferation and accelerate wound closure.
- **Wnt-Activated Biomaterials:** Incorporating Wnt signaling modulators into wound dressings or scaffolds can create a conducive environment for wound healing.

12.2.2 Organ Repair

12.2.2.1 Liver Regeneration

Wnt/β-Catenin signaling is involved in liver regeneration and repair. Activating this pathway can enhance liver recovery after injury or surgery.

- **Gene Delivery for Liver Repair**: Delivery of Wnt ligands or β-Catenin to the liver can promote hepatocyte proliferation and liver regeneration.
- **Wnt Agonists in Liver Disease**: Modulating Wnt signaling in liver diseases such as cirrhosis or hepatitis can improve liver function and repair.

12.2.2.2 Cardiac Repair

Wnt signaling has a role in cardiac repair and regeneration following myocardial infarction.

- **Stem Cell-Based Approaches**: Combining Wnt pathway modulation with stem cell therapy can improve cardiac repair and function after injury.
- **Direct Cardiac Administration**: Local administration of Wnt agonists or gene delivery to the heart can enhance cardiac tissue repair.

12.3 Stem Cell-Based Therapies

Stem cell-based therapies benefit significantly from the modulation of Wnt/β-Catenin signaling, as this pathway is crucial for stem cell self-renewal, differentiation, and tissue regeneration.

12.3.1 Enhancing Stem Cell Self-Renewal

12.3.1.1 Wnt Signaling Activation

Activating Wnt signaling can enhance the self-renewal capacity of stem cells, promoting their expansion and availability for therapeutic applications.

- **Culture Conditions**: Modifying culture conditions with Wnt agonists or β-Catenin stabilizers can improve the yield and quality of stem cells in vitro.

12.3.2 Guiding Stem Cell Differentiation

12.3.2.1 Directed Differentiation

Modulating Wnt signaling can guide the differentiation of stem cells into specific lineages required for tissue repair. For example:

- **Mesenchymal Stem Cells (MSCs)**: Activating Wnt signaling can promote the differentiation of MSCs into osteoblasts for bone repair or cardiomyocytes for cardiac regeneration.
- **Epithelial Stem Cells**: Enhancing Wnt signaling can direct the differentiation of epithelial stem cells into functional epithelial cells for wound healing.

12.3.3 Stem Cell Transplantation

12.3.3.1 Preconditioning Stem Cells

Pre-treating stem cells with Wnt modulators before transplantation can improve their survival, integration, and functionality in the host tissue.

- **In Vivo Activation**: Systemic or localized administration of Wnt agonists in conjunction with stem cell transplantation can enhance the regenerative effects.

12.3.4 Challenges and Future Directions

12.3.4.1 Safety Concerns

Modulating Wnt/β-Catenin signaling carries risks of uncontrolled cell growth and tumorigenesis. Ensuring safety and minimizing adverse effects is crucial for clinical applications.

12.3.4.2 Optimizing Delivery

Developing effective delivery methods for Wnt modulators and stem cells to target tissues is a key challenge. Advanced delivery systems and localized approaches are being explored to address this issue.

12.3.4.3 Personalized Approaches

Tailoring therapies based on individual patient profiles, including genetic and molecular characteristics, can improve the effectiveness of regenerative treatments.

12.3.4.4 Long-Term Outcomes

Understanding the long-term effects of Wnt modulation on tissue repair and stem cell function is essential for developing safe and effective therapies.

Conclusion

Modulating the Wnt/β-Catenin signaling pathway offers significant potential in regenerative medicine, including enhancing tissue repair, improving wound healing, and advancing organ repair and stem cell-based therapies. By leveraging various strategies to activate or inhibit Wnt signaling, researchers and clinicians can improve regenerative outcomes and address a range of medical conditions. Continued research and development are essential to overcome challenges and optimize these therapies for clinical use, with the goal of achieving safe and effective treatments for patients.

CHAPTER THIRTEEN

Novel Insights into Wnt/β-Catenin Signaling

Recent research on the Wnt/β-Catenin signaling pathway has led to significant advancements and new understandings. This chapter explores the latest discoveries and paradigm shifts in Wnt/β-Catenin signaling, its interactions with other signaling pathways, and the technological advancements that have propelled research in this area.

13.1 Recent Discoveries and Paradigm Shifts

Recent discoveries have transformed our understanding of Wnt/β-Catenin signaling, revealing new dimensions to its role in development, disease, and cellular processes.

13.1.1 Non-Canonical Wnt Signaling Pathways

13.1.1.1 Complex Interactions

Emerging evidence highlights that non-canonical Wnt signaling pathways, such as Wnt/PCP (planar cell polarity) and Wnt/Ca2+, are more interconnected with canonical Wnt/β-Catenin signaling than previously thought. These pathways can influence β-Catenin activity and cellular responses.

13.1.1.2 Role in Cellular Dynamics

Non-canonical pathways are now understood to affect cellular processes such as cell migration and polarity, impacting tissue organization and developmental processes.

13.1.2 β-Catenin Dynamics

13.1.2.1 β-Catenin Phosphorylation

Recent studies have identified additional phosphorylation sites on β-Catenin that regulate its stability and activity. For example, phosphorylation at specific serine and threonine residues can influence β-Catenin degradation and transcriptional activity.

13.1.2.2 β-Catenin Function Beyond Transcription

β-Catenin has been found to have non-transcriptional roles, including interactions with cytoskeletal components and involvement in cell-cell adhesion. These functions can affect cellular behavior and tissue integrity.

13.1.3 Wnt Ligand Diversity

13.1.3.1 New Wnt Ligands

Recent discoveries have identified additional Wnt ligands and variants that have unique roles in Wnt signaling. These new ligands may have distinct effects on β-Catenin signaling and cellular responses.

13.1.3.2 Functional Specialization

The functional specialization of Wnt ligands has been demonstrated, where different ligands can activate specific subsets of Wnt signaling pathways and have tissue-specific effects.

13.1.4 Role in Metabolism

13.1.4.1 Wnt Signaling and Metabolic Regulation

Recent research has uncovered a role for Wnt/β-Catenin signaling in regulating metabolic processes, including glucose metabolism and lipid homeostasis. This has implications for understanding metabolic disorders and developing therapeutic strategies.

13.2 Cross-Talk with Other Signaling Pathways

Wnt/β-Catenin signaling does not operate in isolation but interacts with various other signaling pathways. Understanding these interactions provides insights into the complexity of cellular signaling networks and their implications for health and disease.

13.2.1 Wnt/β-Catenin and Hedgehog Signaling

13.2.1.1 Mutual Regulation

Wnt/β-Catenin and Hedgehog signaling pathways can mutually regulate each other. For example, β-Catenin can modulate Hedgehog pathway activity, and vice versa, influencing cellular processes such as stem cell maintenance and tissue regeneration.

13.2.1.2 Co-Activation and Synergy

In some contexts, Wnt and Hedgehog pathways cooperate to enhance signaling outcomes, affecting developmental processes and tissue homeostasis.

13.2.2 Wnt/β-Catenin and Notch Signaling

13.2.2.1 Cross-Talk Mechanisms

The interaction between Wnt/β-Catenin and Notch signaling pathways is crucial for regulating cell fate decisions and tissue patterning. For instance, β-Catenin can influence Notch signaling by modulating the expression of Notch ligands or receptors.

13.2.2.2 Context-Dependent Effects

The effects of Wnt/β-Catenin and Notch signaling can be context-dependent, with their interactions varying across different tissues and developmental stages.

13.2.3 Wnt/β-Catenin and TGF-β Signaling

13.2.3.1 Functional Interplay

Wnt/β-Catenin and TGF-β signaling pathways can interact to regulate processes such as fibrosis and epithelial-mesenchymal transition (EMT). For example, TGF-β signaling can influence Wnt/β-Catenin activity and vice versa, impacting cellular responses in fibrotic diseases and cancer.

13.2.3.2 Regulatory Networks

Understanding how these pathways regulate each other provides insights into complex regulatory networks that control cell behavior and disease progression.

13.2.4 Wnt/β-Catenin and PI3K/Akt Signaling

13.2.4.1 Signal Integration

The interaction between Wnt/β-Catenin and PI3K/Akt signaling pathways integrates growth factor signals with Wnt-mediated effects. This cross-talk can influence cell survival, proliferation, and metabolism.

13.2.4.2 Pathway Crosstalk

Crosstalk between Wnt/β-Catenin and PI3K/Akt pathways can affect the progression of cancer and other diseases, providing potential targets for therapeutic intervention.

13.3 Technological Advancements in Wnt/β-Catenin Research

Advancements in technology have significantly enhanced our ability to study and manipulate Wnt/β-Catenin signaling, leading to new discoveries and therapeutic opportunities.

13.3.1 High-Throughput Screening

13.3.1.1 Drug Discovery

High-throughput screening technologies allow for the identification of small molecules and compounds that modulate Wnt/β-Catenin signaling. These screens can uncover new therapeutic targets and potential drugs for various diseases.

13.3.1.2 Functional Genomics

Advances in functional genomics enable large-scale studies to identify genes and pathways that interact with Wnt/β-Catenin signaling, providing insights into its regulation and function.

13.3.2 CRISPR/Cas9 and Gene Editing

13.3.2.1 Precision Gene Editing

CRISPR/Cas9 technology allows for precise editing of genes involved in Wnt/β-Catenin signaling, enabling detailed studies of their functions and roles in disease.

13.3.2.2 Functional Knockouts and Mutants

Creating knockout or mutant cell lines and animal models helps in understanding the effects of specific genetic modifications on Wnt signaling and related processes.

13.3.3 Single-Cell Technologies

13.3.3.1 Single-Cell RNA Sequencing

Single-cell RNA sequencing provides detailed information about gene expression patterns in individual cells, allowing for the analysis of Wnt/β-Catenin signaling at single-cell resolution.

13.3.3.2 Spatial Transcriptomics

This technology enables the mapping of gene expression within tissue sections, providing insights into the spatial organization of Wnt signaling and its effects on tissue architecture.

13.3.4 Imaging and Reporter Systems

13.3.4.1 Fluorescent Reporters

Advanced imaging techniques using fluorescent reporters, such as TOPflash and FOPflash reporter assays, allow for real-time visualization and quantification of Wnt/β-Catenin signaling activity in living cells and tissues.

13.3.4.2 In Vivo Imaging

Non-invasive imaging techniques, such as bioluminescence and PET imaging, enable the study of Wnt signaling dynamics in living organisms, providing insights into its role in development and disease.

13.3.5 Organoids and 3D Cultures

13.3.5.1 Model Systems

The use of organoids and 3D cell cultures provides more physiologically relevant models for studying Wnt/β-Catenin signaling in complex tissue environments. These models mimic in vivo conditions and facilitate the study of tissue-specific signaling processes.

Conclusion

Recent discoveries and advancements in Wnt/β-Catenin signaling have significantly expanded our understanding of this critical pathway. Paradigm shifts in our knowledge of β-Catenin dynamics, Wnt ligand diversity, and pathway interactions have revealed new aspects of Wnt signaling's role in development and disease. Cross-talk with other signaling pathways, such as Hedgehog, Notch, TGF-β, and PI3K/Akt, underscores the complexity of cellular signaling networks. Technological advancements, including high-throughput screening, CRISPR/Cas9 gene editing, single-cell technologies, and advanced imaging, have provided powerful tools for studying and manipulating Wnt/β-Catenin signaling. These developments hold promise for uncovering new therapeutic opportunities and improving our understanding of Wnt signaling's role in health and disease.

CHAPTER FOURTEEN

Future Prospects and Challenges

As research on the Wnt/β-Catenin signaling pathway continues to advance, new therapeutic strategies and research directions are emerging. However, several challenges remain that must be addressed to fully harness the potential of this pathway in treating diseases and advancing personalized medicine. This chapter explores the future prospects and challenges in the field of Wnt/β-Catenin signaling.

14.1 Emerging Therapeutic Strategies

The potential for therapeutic intervention targeting the Wnt/β-Catenin pathway is vast, with numerous strategies being explored to address various diseases, including cancer, degenerative disorders, and metabolic conditions.

14.1.1 Small Molecule Modulators

14.1.1.1 Wnt Activators

Small molecules that activate Wnt signaling, such as **GSK-3β inhibitors** and **Wnt agonists**, are being developed to promote tissue regeneration and repair. These molecules can enhance β-Catenin stability and transcriptional activity, potentially treating conditions like osteoporosis and muscle degeneration.

14.1.1.2 Wnt Inhibitors

Conversely, small molecules that inhibit Wnt signaling, such as **Wnt antagonists** or **CK1 inhibitors**, are being explored for cancer therapy. These inhibitors aim to block aberrant Wnt signaling associated with tumor progression and metastasis.

14.1.2 Biological Therapeutics

14.1.2.1 Monoclonal Antibodies

Antibodies targeting specific components of the Wnt/β-Catenin pathway, such as **Dkk1** or **Frizzled receptors**, are being developed to modulate pathway activity. These biologics have potential applications in treating diseases like cancer and bone disorders.

14.1.2.2 Peptides and Fusion Proteins

Engineered peptides and fusion proteins that interfere with Wnt/β-Catenin signaling are being tested for therapeutic use. These biologics can selectively target and inhibit specific interactions within the pathway.

14.1.3 Gene Therapy

14.1.3.1 Gene Delivery

Techniques for delivering genes encoding Wnt ligands, β-Catenin, or pathway inhibitors are being explored to modulate Wnt signaling in vivo. Gene therapy approaches aim to correct or enhance Wnt signaling in target tissues or cells.

14.1.3.2 CRISPR/Cas9

Gene editing technologies like CRISPR/Cas9 are being used to create precise modifications in genes related to Wnt signaling. This approach allows for targeted manipulation of the pathway and holds promise for treating genetic disorders and cancers.

14.1.4 Cell-Based Therapies

14.1.4.1 Stem Cell Therapy

Combining Wnt pathway modulation with stem cell therapy can enhance tissue regeneration and repair. Strategies include pre-treating stem cells with Wnt modulators before transplantation or administering Wnt agonists to promote stem cell differentiation and function.

14.1.4.2 Tissue Engineering

Wnt signaling is being integrated into tissue engineering approaches to develop functional tissues and organs. Modulating Wnt pathways can improve the development and integration of engineered tissues.

14.2 Unresolved Questions in Wnt Signaling

Despite significant progress, several unresolved questions remain regarding Wnt/β-Catenin signaling that need to be addressed to advance the field.

14.2.1 Mechanistic Details

14.2.1.1 β-Catenin Regulation

While the core components of Wnt/β-Catenin signaling are well understood, the precise mechanisms regulating β-Catenin stability, localization, and transcriptional activity are not fully elucidated. Further research is needed to clarify these mechanisms and their implications for cellular processes.

14.2.1.2 Ligand-Receptor Interactions

The interactions between different Wnt ligands and their receptors are complex and not completely understood. Determining how specific Wnt ligands activate distinct pathways and the functional consequences of these interactions is crucial.

14.2.2 Context-Dependent Effects

14.2.2.1 Tissue-Specific Functions

Wnt/β-Catenin signaling has context-dependent effects in different tissues and developmental stages. Understanding how the pathway operates in various cellular and tissue contexts will help in designing targeted therapies and predicting outcomes.

14.2.2.2 Pathway Crosstalk

The interactions between Wnt/β-Catenin signaling and other pathways (e.g., Notch, TGF-β) are complex. Further studies are needed to elucidate how these pathways integrate and influence each other in different biological processes and diseases.

14.2.3 Therapeutic Challenges

14.2.3.1 Specificity and Off-Target Effects

Developing therapeutic agents that selectively target Wnt/β-Catenin signaling components without affecting other pathways is challenging. Ensuring specificity and minimizing off-target effects are critical for the safety and efficacy of therapeutic interventions.

14.2.3.2 Resistance and Adaptation

Tumor cells and other disease states can develop resistance to therapies targeting Wnt/β-Catenin signaling. Understanding mechanisms of resistance and identifying strategies to overcome it will be essential for the long-term success of these therapies.

14.3 Potential for Personalized Medicine

The potential for personalized medicine in the context of Wnt/β-Catenin signaling lies in tailoring treatments based on individual genetic, molecular, and clinical profiles.

14.3.1 Genetic and Molecular Profiling

14.3.1.1 Patient Stratification

Genetic and molecular profiling of patients can identify specific mutations or alterations in Wnt signaling components. This information can be used to stratify patients and tailor treatments based on their individual profiles.

14.3.1.2 Biomarker Development

Identifying biomarkers associated with Wnt/β-Catenin signaling activity can help in predicting patient responses to therapies and monitoring treatment efficacy.

14.3.2 Customized Therapeutic Approaches

14.3.2.1 Targeted Therapies

Personalized approaches involve developing and applying therapies that target specific components of the Wnt/β-Catenin pathway based on individual patient profiles. This includes selecting the most appropriate small molecules, biologics, or gene therapies for each patient.

14.3.2.2 Precision Medicine in Cancer

Personalized medicine can optimize the use of Wnt/β-Catenin pathway inhibitors or activators in cancer treatment. Tailoring therapies to the molecular characteristics of individual tumors can improve outcomes and reduce adverse effects.

14.3.3 Patient-Specific Models

14.3.3.1 Organoids and Patient-Derived Models

Creating patient-derived organoids or other models can help in studying the effects of Wnt/β-Catenin signaling in a personalized context. These models allow for testing therapies in a system that closely mimics the patient's condition.

14.3.3.2 Drug Screening and Optimization

Personalized models can be used to screen for and optimize drugs based on individual patient profiles, ensuring that the most effective and safest therapies are identified.

Conclusion

The future of Wnt/β-Catenin signaling research holds promising therapeutic opportunities and the potential for personalized medicine. Emerging therapeutic strategies, including small molecules, biological therapeutics, gene therapy, and cell-based approaches, offer exciting possibilities for treating a range of diseases. However, unresolved questions regarding the mechanistic details of Wnt signaling, context-dependent effects, and therapeutic challenges need to be addressed. The potential for personalized medicine, driven by genetic and molecular profiling, offers a pathway to tailor treatments to individual patient profiles, improving outcomes and advancing the field. Continued research and development are essential to overcome these challenges and fully realize the potential of Wnt/β-Catenin signaling in therapeutic applications.

CHAPTER FIFTEEN

Case Studies and Clinical Applications

This chapter focuses on the application of Wnt/β-Catenin pathway research to clinical settings through case studies and examples. It highlights the role of this signaling pathway in various diseases and the translation of basic research findings into practical clinical applications.

15.1 Case Studies Illustrating Wnt/β-Catenin Pathway's Role in Various Diseases

15.1.1 Cancer

15.1.1.1 Colorectal Cancer

Case Study: A patient with metastatic colorectal cancer showed significant β-Catenin mutations leading to uncontrolled Wnt signaling. Targeted therapies such as **Porcupine inhibitors** and **Frizzled receptor antagonists** were explored in clinical trials to manage this patient's disease.

Clinical Findings: Patients with β-Catenin mutations had poorer prognoses and showed partial responses to targeted therapies. Research into combination therapies is ongoing to improve efficacy and overcome resistance.

15.1.1.2 Breast Cancer

Case Study: In a cohort of patients with triple-negative breast cancer, elevated Wnt/β-Catenin signaling was associated with poor outcomes. Researchers investigated the use of **Wnt signaling inhibitors** in combination with standard chemotherapy.

Clinical Findings: Some patients experienced increased sensitivity to chemotherapy and reduced tumor growth with Wnt inhibitors. However, challenges in patient stratification and side effects required further investigation.

15.1.1.3 Liver Cancer

Case Study: A patient with hepatocellular carcinoma (HCC) was found to have aberrant Wnt/β-Catenin signaling due to mutations in **CTNNB1** (β-Catenin gene). Clinical trials tested the efficacy of **targeted small molecules** against Wnt signaling.

Clinical Findings: While some tumors showed a reduction in size, long-term efficacy was limited by the development of resistance and the heterogeneity of the tumors.

15.1.2 Osteoporosis

Case Study: In a study of patients with osteoporosis, reduced Wnt signaling was linked to decreased bone density. **Wnt agonists** such as **Sclerostin inhibitors** were used to enhance bone formation in clinical trials.

Clinical Findings: Patients treated with Wnt agonists showed improvements in bone density and reduced fracture rates. However, ongoing monitoring for potential side effects and long-term outcomes is necessary.

15.1.3 Metabolic Disorders

Case Study: Patients with type 2 diabetes were observed to have altered Wnt/β-Catenin signaling, affecting insulin sensitivity. Clinical trials investigated the use of **Wnt pathway modulators** to improve metabolic control.

Clinical Findings: Some patients demonstrated improved insulin sensitivity and glycemic control with Wnt modulators. Challenges include optimizing dosing and managing side effects associated with pathway modulation.

15.1.4 Neurodegenerative Diseases

Case Study: In patients with Alzheimer's disease, altered Wnt/β-Catenin signaling was observed. Clinical trials tested **Wnt pathway activators** to counteract neurodegeneration and cognitive decline.

Clinical Findings: Preliminary results indicated potential benefits in cognitive function, though the therapy's effectiveness varied among patients. Further studies are required to understand the long-term effects and safety.

15.2 Translation of Basic Research to Clinical Applications

Translating basic research findings on Wnt/β-Catenin signaling into clinical applications involves several critical steps, including preclinical research, clinical trials, and regulatory approval.

15.2.1 Preclinical Research

15.2.1.1 Animal Models

Basic research utilizing animal models has provided valuable insights into Wnt/β-Catenin signaling mechanisms and their role in disease. For example, genetically engineered mice with aberrant Wnt signaling have been instrumental in studying cancer and bone diseases.

15.2.1.2 Cell-Based Assays

Research using cell-based assays has identified potential therapeutic targets within the Wnt pathway. These assays help in screening compounds and assessing their effects on Wnt signaling and cellular outcomes.

15.2.2 Clinical Trials

15.2.2.1 Phase I Trials

Initial clinical trials focus on assessing the safety, dosage, and tolerability of new Wnt-targeted therapies. For instance, early trials of Wnt inhibitors and agonists have evaluated their safety profiles and dose-related side effects.

15.2.2.2 Phase II Trials

Subsequent trials aim to determine the efficacy of Wnt-targeted therapies in specific patient populations. Trials in cancer, osteoporosis, and metabolic disorders have provided preliminary data on therapeutic benefits and challenges.

15.2.2.3 Phase III Trials

Large-scale trials are conducted to confirm the efficacy and safety of therapies across diverse populations. These trials often include multiple centers and extensive patient cohorts to validate clinical outcomes and refine therapeutic approaches.

15.2.3 Regulatory Approval

15.2.3.1 FDA and EMA Regulations

Regulatory bodies such as the FDA (U.S. Food and Drug Administration) and EMA (European Medicines Agency) review clinical trial data to approve new therapies. Successful translation of Wnt-targeted therapies into clinical use requires comprehensive data on safety, efficacy, and manufacturing.

15.2.3.2 Market Access

Once approved, therapies must navigate market access, including pricing, reimbursement, and distribution. Collaboration with healthcare providers and stakeholders ensures that new therapies reach patients effectively.

15.2.4 Personalized Medicine

15.2.4.1 Biomarker Development

Identifying biomarkers associated with Wnt/β-Catenin signaling helps in personalizing treatment. Biomarkers can predict patient responses to therapies and guide treatment decisions.

15.2.4.2 Tailored Therapies

Personalized approaches involve customizing therapies based on individual patient profiles, including genetic and molecular characteristics. This approach improves treatment outcomes and minimizes adverse effects.

Conclusion

This Chapter underscores the importance of translating Wnt/β-Catenin pathway research into clinical applications through detailed case studies and practical examples. The role of Wnt signaling in various diseases demonstrates its therapeutic potential, with ongoing research focusing on refining and optimizing treatment strategies. Translational efforts involve rigorous preclinical research, clinical trials, and regulatory processes to ensure the safety and efficacy of new therapies. The integration of personalized medicine further enhances the potential of Wnt-targeted therapies by tailoring treatments to individual patient needs. As research advances, continued collaboration between basic scientists, clinicians, and regulatory agencies will be essential in realizing the full potential of Wnt/β-Catenin signaling in clinical practice.

CHAPTER SIXTEEN

Techniques to Study Wnt/β-Catenin Pathway

Understanding the Wnt/β-Catenin signaling pathway involves a variety of experimental techniques and models to elucidate its mechanisms, interactions, and roles in disease. This chapter provides a detailed account of the techniques used to study the Wnt/β-Catenin pathway, covering in vitro and in vivo models, imaging and molecular biology techniques, and high-throughput screening methods.

16.1 In Vitro Models

16.1.1 Cell Line Models

16.1.1.1 Wnt Reporter Cell Lines

These cell lines are engineered to express reporter genes (e.g., GFP, luciferase) under the control of Wnt-responsive promoters (e.g., TOPFLASH or FOPFLASH reporters). They are used to measure Wnt pathway activation and screen for pathway modulators.

16.1.1.2 Knockout/Knockdown Cell Lines

Techniques like CRISPR/Cas9 or RNA interference (RNAi) are used to create cell lines with specific genetic alterations in Wnt pathway components (e.g., β-Catenin, Frizzled receptors). These models help in studying the functional consequences of these alterations.

16.1.2 Primary Cell Cultures

16.1.2.1 Stem Cells

Primary stem cells, including embryonic stem cells (ESCs) and induced pluripotent stem cells (iPSCs), are used to study Wnt signaling in developmental and regenerative contexts. These cells can be differentiated into various cell types to investigate tissue-specific Wnt functions.

16.1.2.2 Primary Tissue Cultures

Cultures derived from specific tissues (e.g., intestinal epithelial cells, fibroblasts) are used to study the localized effects of Wnt signaling and the interactions between Wnt signaling and tissue-specific processes.

16.1.3 3D Cell Culture Systems

16.1.3.1 Organoids

These are 3D cultures that mimic the architecture and function of organs. Wnt signaling is crucial for the development and maintenance of organoids, making them valuable for studying tissue development, regeneration, and disease modeling.

16.1.3.2 Spheroids

Tumor spheroids are used to study the effects of Wnt signaling in a more physiologically relevant environment compared to traditional 2D cultures. They provide insights into tumor microenvironment interactions and drug responses.

16.2 In Vivo Models

16.2.1 Genetically Engineered Mice

16.2.1.1 Knockout Mice

Mice with specific genes (e.g., β-Catenin, APC) knocked out are used to study the physiological roles of these genes and their involvement in disease. These models help in understanding the systemic effects of Wnt signaling disruptions.

16.2.1.2 Transgenic Mice

Mice engineered to express mutant forms of Wnt signaling components (e.g., stabilized β-Catenin) provide insights into how altered Wnt signaling contributes to disease processes, such as cancer and developmental disorders.

16.2.2 Conditional Knockout Mice

16.2.2.1 Tissue-Specific Knockouts

These models allow researchers to study Wnt signaling in specific tissues or developmental stages by using Cre-LoxP technology to conditionally delete genes in response to specific stimuli or at certain times.

16.2.3 Xenograft Models

16.2.3.1 Human Tumor Xenografts

Human cancer cells are implanted into immunocompromised mice to study the role of Wnt signaling in tumor growth and response to therapies. These models help in evaluating the efficacy of Wnt-targeted treatments.

16.3 Imaging Techniques

16.3.1 Fluorescence Microscopy

16.3.1.1 Confocal Microscopy

Provides high-resolution images of cellular structures and Wnt signaling components within live or fixed cells. Confocal microscopy is used to visualize the localization and dynamics of Wnt pathway proteins.

16.3.1.2 Fluorescence Resonance Energy Transfer (FRET)

Used to study protein-protein interactions and dynamic changes in Wnt signaling in live cells. FRET allows researchers to monitor real-time interactions between Wnt signaling components.

16.3.2 Immunohistochemistry (IHC) and Immunofluorescence

16.3.2.1 IHC

Utilizes antibodies to detect Wnt signaling proteins in tissue sections. IHC provides information on protein localization, expression levels, and tissue distribution.

16.3.2.2 Immunofluorescence

Uses fluorescently labeled antibodies to visualize the distribution and colocalization of Wnt signaling components in cells and tissues.

16.3.3 Live Cell Imaging

16.3.3.1 Time-Lapse Microscopy

Allows researchers to monitor dynamic processes involving Wnt signaling in living cells over time. This technique is useful for studying changes in cellular morphology, signaling dynamics, and response to stimuli.

16.4 Molecular Biology Techniques

16.4.1 Western Blotting

16.4.1.1 Protein Analysis

Western blotting is used to detect and quantify Wnt signaling proteins and their post-translational modifications. This technique helps in assessing changes in protein expression and signaling pathway activation.

16.4.2 Quantitative PCR (qPCR)

16.4.2.1 Gene Expression Analysis

qPCR is used to measure the expression levels of Wnt signaling-related genes. It provides insights into the transcriptional regulation of Wnt pathway components.

16.4.3 Chromatin Immunoprecipitation (ChIP)

16.4.3.1 Transcriptional Regulation

ChIP assays are used to study the interaction of Wnt/β-Catenin with DNA and its effects on gene expression. This technique helps in identifying target genes regulated by Wnt signaling.

16.4.4 Reporter Assays

16.4.4.1 Wnt Reporter Assays

Utilizes reporter constructs (e.g., luciferase or GFP) driven by Wnt-responsive promoters to measure Wnt pathway activity. These assays are used in screening for pathway modulators and understanding the effects of various treatments.

16.5 High-Throughput Screening (HTS) Methods

16.5.1 Small Molecule Screens

16.5.1.1 Chemical Libraries

HTS involves screening large chemical libraries for compounds that modulate Wnt signaling. This approach identifies potential drugs that can either activate or inhibit the pathway.

16.5.1.2 Assay Development

HTS assays are developed using Wnt reporter cell lines or biochemical assays to screen for compounds with desired effects on Wnt signaling.

16.5.2 siRNA and shRNA Screens

16.5.2.1 Gene Knockdown Screens

HTS screens using small interfering RNA (siRNA) or short hairpin RNA (shRNA) libraries to knock down Wnt pathway components. These screens identify genes that are essential for Wnt signaling and potential therapeutic targets.

16.5.3 Protein-Protein Interaction Screens

16.5.3.1 Yeast Two-Hybrid

This technique is used to identify protein interactions within the Wnt/β-Catenin pathway. Yeast two-hybrid screens help in discovering novel pathway components and interaction partners.

16.5.3.2 Co-Immunoprecipitation (Co-IP)

Co-IP assays are used to study protein complexes and interactions within the Wnt pathway. This technique provides insights into the molecular mechanisms of Wnt signaling.

16.5.4 Genomic Screens

16.5.4.1 CRISPR/Cas9 Screens

High-throughput CRISPR screens are used to identify genes involved in Wnt signaling and their roles in various cellular processes. This approach allows for the systematic exploration of gene functions and pathway regulation.

Conclusion

This chapter provides a comprehensive overview of the techniques used to study the Wnt/β-Catenin signaling pathway. In vitro and in vivo models offer valuable insights into the pathway's roles in development, disease, and therapy. Imaging and molecular biology techniques allow researchers to visualize and analyze pathway components, interactions, and dynamics. High-throughput screening methods enable the identification of novel modulators and therapeutic targets. Together, these techniques contribute to a deeper understanding of Wnt signaling and its potential applications in research and clinical settings.

CHAPTER SEVENTEEN

Computational Modeling of Wnt/β-Catenin Signaling

Computational modeling has become an essential tool in understanding the complex dynamics of the Wnt/β-Catenin signaling pathway. This chapter explores various computational approaches used to study and predict the behavior of this pathway, including bioinformatics approaches, systems biology models, and predictive modeling in drug discovery.

17.1 Bioinformatics Approaches

17.1.1 Database Resources

17.1.1.1 Wnt Pathway Databases

WntDB: A specialized database providing information on Wnt signaling components, interactions, and functional annotations. Researchers use it to gather data on Wnt-related genes, proteins, and their roles in signaling.

KEGG Pathway Database: Offers detailed maps of signaling pathways, including Wnt/β-Catenin. This database helps researchers visualize the pathway components and their interactions.

17.1.1.2 Protein-Protein Interaction Databases

STRING: Provides a comprehensive repository of known and predicted protein-protein interactions. This resource helps identify potential interaction partners within the Wnt signaling network.

BioGRID: A database that contains curated protein interaction data, including interactions related to the Wnt/β-Catenin pathway.

17.1.2 Sequence Analysis

17.1.2.1 Gene and Protein Sequence Databases

NCBI GenBank: Contains nucleotide and protein sequence data. Researchers use GenBank to obtain sequences of Wnt pathway components for analysis and comparison.

UniProt: Provides detailed protein sequence and functional information, including post-translational modifications relevant to Wnt signaling.

17.1.2.2 Sequence Alignment and Homology

BLAST: Used for sequence alignment to identify homologous genes and proteins involved in Wnt signaling. BLAST helps in understanding evolutionary relationships and functional conservation.

Clustal Omega: A tool for multiple sequence alignment, which aids in identifying conserved regions and functional domains within Wnt pathway proteins.

17.1.3 Functional Annotation

17.1.3.1 Gene Ontology (GO)

GO Term Enrichment: GO annotations provide information on the biological processes, cellular components, and molecular functions of Wnt pathway genes. Enrichment analysis helps identify the functional roles of these genes in signaling and disease.

DAVID Bioinformatics Resources: Used to perform functional annotation and enrichment analysis of gene lists related to Wnt signaling.

17.1.3.2 Pathway Analysis Tools

Reactome: Offers curated pathways and interactions, including Wnt signaling. Reactome helps researchers understand the pathway's role in cellular processes and diseases.

Pathway Commons: Aggregates data from multiple sources to provide a comprehensive view of signaling pathways, including Wnt/β-Catenin.

17.2 Systems Biology Models

17.2.1 Network Modeling

17.2.1.1 Interaction Networks

Protein-Protein Interaction Networks: Network models visualize the interactions between Wnt signaling proteins, including their upstream regulators and downstream effectors. Tools like Cytoscape are used to create and analyze these networks.

Gene Regulatory Networks: Models depicting the regulatory relationships between Wnt signaling components and target genes. These networks help understand how Wnt signaling influences gene expression.

17.2.1.2 Pathway Simulation

Boolean Networks: Simplified models representing the on/off states of pathway components. Boolean networks are used to simulate and predict the behavior of Wnt signaling under various conditions.

Dynamic Network Models: Incorporate time-dependent changes in signaling components to simulate the temporal dynamics of Wnt signaling. These models help understand how signaling changes over time and in response to stimuli.

17.2.2 Computational Approaches

17.2.2.1 Ordinary Differential Equations (ODEs)

Mathematical Modeling: ODEs are used to describe the kinetics of Wnt signaling components and their interactions. These models help quantify the rate of changes in signaling molecules and predict pathway dynamics.

Simulation Tools: Software such as MATLAB and COPASI are used to solve ODE models and simulate the behavior of Wnt signaling under different conditions.

17.2.2.2 Agent-Based Models

Individual-Based Simulation: Agent-based models simulate the behavior of individual cells or molecules within the Wnt signaling network. These models help explore how local interactions contribute to overall pathway dynamics.

17.2.2.3 Stochastic Models

Probabilistic Modeling: Stochastic models account for random fluctuations in signaling components and their effects on pathway behavior. These models are useful for studying variability and uncertainty in Wnt signaling.

17.2.3 Data Integration

17.2.3.1 Multi-Omics Integration

Integration of Genomic, Transcriptomic, and Proteomic Data: Combining data from various omics technologies provides a comprehensive view of Wnt signaling. Integration helps in identifying key regulatory nodes and pathways affected by Wnt signaling.

Tools for Data Integration: Software like Integrative Genomics Viewer (IGV) and Multi-Omics Factor Analysis (MOFA) are used to analyze and visualize integrated omics data.

17.2.3.2 Machine Learning Approaches

Predictive Modeling: Machine learning algorithms are used to analyze large datasets and identify patterns related to Wnt signaling. Techniques such as clustering, classification, and regression help in predicting pathway behavior and drug responses.

17.3 Predictive Modeling in Drug Discovery

17.3.1 Target Identification and Validation

17.3.1.1 Bioinformatics Tools

Ligand-Receptor Interaction Prediction: Tools like AutoDock and Glide are used to predict interactions between potential drugs and Wnt pathway components. These predictions help identify promising drug targets.

Molecular Docking: Docking simulations help in understanding how small molecules interact with Wnt signaling proteins and assess their potential as therapeutic agents.

17.3.1.2 Target Validation

Experimental Validation: Computational predictions are validated through experimental assays to confirm the efficacy of drug candidates in modulating Wnt signaling. Techniques include in vitro assays and in vivo studies.

17.3.2 Drug Screening and Optimization

17.3.2.1 Virtual Screening

High-Throughput Virtual Screening: Utilizes computational models to screen large libraries of compounds for activity against Wnt signaling components. Virtual screening accelerates the drug discovery process by identifying potential candidates.

Pharmacophore Modeling: Models the essential features of drugs that interact with Wnt signaling targets. Pharmacophore models help design new compounds with desired biological activity.

17.3.2.2 Lead Optimization

Molecular Dynamics (MD) Simulations: MD simulations are used to refine drug candidates by studying their stability and interactions with Wnt signaling targets over time. This helps in optimizing lead compounds for better efficacy and reduced side effects.

Quantitative Structure-Activity Relationship (QSAR) Modeling: QSAR models predict the activity of drug candidates based on their chemical structure. These models guide the optimization of compounds to enhance their interaction with Wnt signaling targets.

17.3.3 Clinical Translation

17.3.3.1 Predictive Biomarkers

Biomarker Discovery: Computational models help identify biomarkers associated with Wnt signaling that can predict patient responses to treatments. These biomarkers guide clinical trial design and patient stratification.

Personalized Medicine: Predictive models are used to tailor treatments based on individual patient profiles, improving the efficacy of Wnt-targeted therapies.

17.3.3.2 Risk Assessment

Safety and Efficacy Predictions: Computational models help assess the safety and efficacy of drug candidates before clinical trials. These predictions reduce the risk of adverse effects and increase the likelihood of successful drug development.

Conclusion

This chapter delves into the computational techniques used to study and model the Wnt/β-Catenin signaling pathway. Bioinformatics approaches provide essential data and insights into the components and interactions within the pathway. Systems biology models offer a framework for understanding the dynamic and complex nature of Wnt signaling, while predictive modeling in drug discovery accelerates the identification and optimization of therapeutic agents. These computational tools and models play a crucial role in advancing our understanding of Wnt signaling and translating research findings into clinical applications.

Glossary Of Terms

Adenomatous Polyposis Coli (APC)

A tumor suppressor protein that is a key component of the Wnt/β-Catenin destruction complex. It helps regulate β-Catenin levels by promoting its degradation.

β-Catenin

A central protein in the Wnt signaling pathway that acts as a transcriptional co-activator. When stabilized, it translocates to the nucleus and activates Wnt target genes.

Canonical Wnt Signaling

The primary Wnt signaling pathway that involves the stabilization and nuclear accumulation of β-Catenin, leading to the activation of TCF/LEF transcription factors.

Co-receptors

Proteins that work with Wnt receptors to facilitate signaling. Key co-receptors in the Wnt/β-Catenin pathway include LRP5 and LRP6.

Destruction Complex

A protein complex that includes APC, Axin, Glycogen Synthase Kinase 3 Beta (GSK-3β), and Casein Kinase 1 (CK1). This complex regulates β-Catenin degradation in the absence of Wnt signaling.

Frizzled Receptors

A family of G protein-coupled receptors that bind Wnt ligands. They play a crucial role in transmitting Wnt signals into the cell.

Gene Ontology (GO)

A framework for the functional annotation of genes and gene products, including the biological processes, molecular functions, and cellular components associated with Wnt signaling components.

Glycogen Synthase Kinase 3 Beta (GSK-3β)

A kinase involved in the destruction complex that phosphorylates β-Catenin, marking it for degradation.

High-Throughput Screening

A method used to quickly conduct millions of chemical, genetic, or pharmacological tests to identify active compounds, antibodies, or genes that modulate Wnt signaling.

LRP5/6 (Low-Density Lipoprotein Receptor-Related Protein 5/6)

Co-receptors that interact with Frizzled receptors and Wnt ligands to propagate Wnt signaling.

Non-Canonical Wnt Signaling

Alternative Wnt signaling pathways that do not involve β-Catenin stabilization, such as the Wnt/Ca2+ pathway and the Wnt/Planar Cell Polarity (PCP) pathway.

Nuclear Transcription Factors

Proteins that bind to specific DNA sequences to regulate gene expression. In the Wnt/β-Catenin pathway, TCF/LEF are key transcription factors activated by β-Catenin.

Planar Cell Polarity (PCP) Pathway

A non-canonical Wnt signaling pathway involved in regulating cell orientation and organization within the plane of a tissue.

Stem Cells

Undifferentiated cells with the potential to develop into various cell types. Wnt/β-Catenin signaling is crucial for maintaining stem cell populations and regulating their differentiation.

TCF/LEF Transcription Factors

Transcription factors that partner with β-Catenin in the nucleus to drive the expression of Wnt target genes. TCF (T-cell factor) and LEF (lymphoid enhancer factor) are key components in the canonical Wnt pathway.

Tumor Suppressor Genes

Genes that encode proteins which help regulate cell growth and prevent uncontrolled cell division. In the context of Wnt signaling, APC is a well-known tumor suppressor.

Wnt Ligands

A family of secreted signaling molecules that bind to Frizzled receptors and initiate Wnt signaling. Wnt ligands are crucial for activating the Wnt/β-Catenin pathway.

Wnt Signaling Pathway

A complex network of proteins involved in cell-to-cell communication that regulates various developmental processes and cellular functions. It is classified into canonical (β-Catenin-dependent) and non-canonical (β-Catenin-independent) pathways.

Wnt/β-Catenin Destruction Complex

A multi-protein complex that controls the degradation of β-Catenin in the absence of Wnt signaling. Components include APC, Axin, GSK-3β, and CK1.

Systems Biology Models

Computational models that integrate experimental data to understand complex biological systems, including signaling pathways like Wnt/β-Catenin.

Bioinformatics

The application of computational tools and techniques to analyze biological data, such as gene sequences and protein interactions, in the context of Wnt signaling research.

Computational Modeling

The use of mathematical and computational methods to simulate and predict the behavior of biological systems, including signaling pathways.

Pharmacophore Modeling

A computational technique used to identify the essential features of molecules that are necessary for interaction with a specific target, such as Wnt signaling components.

Lead Optimization

The process of improving the properties of a lead compound to enhance its efficacy, selectivity, and safety as a therapeutic agent targeting Wnt signaling.

Gene Therapy

A therapeutic approach that involves modifying or introducing genes into a patient's cells to treat or prevent disease. In the context of Wnt signaling, gene therapy may aim to correct signaling defects.

Small Molecule Inhibitors

Chemical compounds that specifically inhibit the activity of Wnt signaling components, used as potential therapeutic agents to modulate the pathway.

Molecular Dynamics (MD) Simulations

Computational simulations that study the physical movements of atoms and molecules, helping to understand the interactions of drug candidates with Wnt signaling proteins.

Predictive Modeling

The use of computational models to predict the outcomes of drug treatments and other interventions based on known data and biological mechanisms.

Personalized Medicine

An approach to healthcare that tailors medical treatment to the individual characteristics of each patient, including their genetic profile, which may involve targeting specific pathways like Wnt/β-Catenin.

Biomarker Discovery

The identification of biological molecules that indicate the presence or progression of disease and can be used to guide treatment decisions, including those related to Wnt signaling.

www.ingramcontent.com/pod-product-compliance
Ingram Content Group UK Ltd.
Pitfield, Milton Keynes, MK11 3LW, UK
UKHW062008290726
14090UKWH00022B/1456